PRIMARY

Problem-solving in mathematics

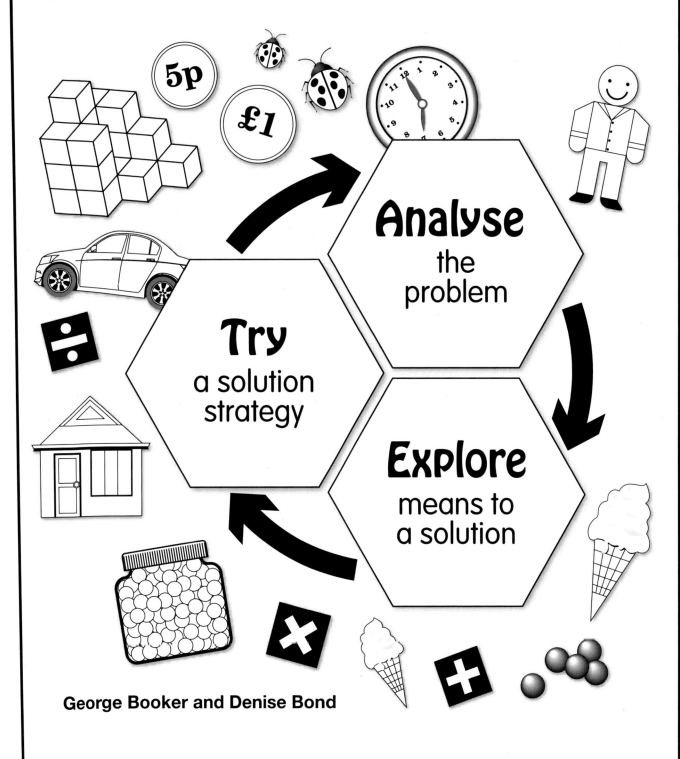

- Analyse the problem
- Explore means to a solution
- Try a solution strategy

George Booker and Denise Bond

6031UK

Problem-solving in mathematics *(Book B)*

Published by R.I.C. Publications® 2008

Republished under licence by Prim-Ed Publishing 2009

Copyright© George Booker and Denise Bond 2007

ISBN 978-1-84654-183-4

PR–6031

Titles available in this series:
Problem-solving in mathematics *(Book A)*
Problem-solving in mathematics *(Book B)*
Problem-solving in mathematics *(Book C)*
Problem-solving in mathematics *(Book D)*
Problem-solving in mathematics *(Book E)*
Problem-solving in mathematics *(Book F)*
Problem-solving in mathematics *(Book G)*

Internet websites

In some cases, websites or specific URLs may be recommended. While these are checked and rechecked at the time of publication, the publisher has no control over any subsequent changes which may be made to webpages. It is *strongly* recommended that the class teacher checks *all* URLs before allowing pupils to access them.

View all pages online

Website: www.prim-ed.com

Books A–G of *Problem-solving in mathematics* have been developed to provide a rich resource for teachers of pupils from the early years to the end of primary school and into secondary school. The series of problems, discussions of ways to understand what is being asked and means of obtaining solutions have been built up to improve the problem-solving performance and persistence of all pupils. It is a fundamental belief of the authors that it is critical that pupils and teachers engage with a few complex problems over an extended period rather than spend a short time on many straightforward 'problems' or exercises. In particular, it is essential to allow pupils time to review and discuss what is required in the problem-solving process before moving to another and different problem. This book includes extensive ideas for extending problems and solution strategies to assist teachers in implementing this vital aspect of mathematics in their classrooms. Also, the problems have been constructed and selected over many years' experience with pupils at all levels of mathematical talent and persistence, as well as in discussions with teachers in classrooms and professional learning and university settings.

Problem-solving does not come easily to most people, so learners need many experiences engaging with problems if they are to develop this crucial ability. As they grapple with problem meaning and find solutions, pupils will learn a great deal about mathematics and mathematical reasoning—for instance, how to organise information to uncover meanings and allow connections among the various facets of a problem to become more apparent, leading to a focus on organising what needs to be done rather than simply looking to apply one or more strategies. In turn, this extended thinking will help pupils make informed choices about events that affect their lives and to interpret and respond to the decisions made by others at school, in everyday life and in further study.

Pupil and teacher pages

The pupil pages present problems chosen with a particular problem-solving focus and draw on a range of mathematical understandings and processes. For each set of related problems, teacher notes and discussion are provided, as well as indications of how particular problems can be examined and solved. Answers to the more straightforward problems and detailed solutions to the more complex problems

ensure appropriate explanations, and suggest ways in which problems can be extended. Related problems occur on one or more pages that extend the problem's ideas, the solution processes and pupils' understanding of the range of ways to come to terms with what the problems are asking.

At the top of each teacher page, a statement highlights the particular thinking that the problems will demand, together with an indication of the mathematics that might be needed and a list of materials that can be used in seeking a solution. A particular focus for the page or set of three pages of problems then expands on these aspects. Each book is organised so that when a problem requires complicated strategic thinking, two or three problems occur on one page (supported by a teacher page with detailed discussion) to encourage pupils to find a solution together with a range of means that can be followed. More often, problems are grouped as a series of three interrelated pages where the level of complexity gradually increases, while the associated teacher page examines one or two of the problems in depth and highlights how the other problems might be solved in a similar manner.

Each teacher page concludes with two further aspects critical to the successful teaching of problem-solving. A section on likely difficulties points to reasoning and content inadequacies that experience has shown may well impede pupils' success. In this way, teachers can be on the lookout for difficulties and be prepared to guide pupils past these potential pitfalls. The final section suggests extensions to the problems to enable teachers to provide several related experiences with problems of these kinds in order to build a rich array of experiences with particular solution methods; for example, the numbers, shapes or measurements in the original problems might change but leave the means to a solution essentially the same, or the context may change while the numbers, shapes or measurements remain the same. Then numbers, shapes or measurements *and* the context could be changed to see how the pupils handle situations that appear different but are essentially the same as those already met and solved.

Other suggestions ask pupils to make and pose their own problems, investigate and present background to the problems or topics to the class, or consider solutions at a more general level (possibly involving verbal descriptions and eventually pictorial or symbolic arguments). In this way, not only are pupils' ways of thinking extended but the problems written on one page are used to produce several more problems that utilise the same approach.

Mathematics and language

The difficulty of the mathematics gradually increases over the series, largely in line with what is taught at the various year levels, although problem-solving both challenges at the point of the mathematics that is being learned and provides insights and motivation for what might be learned next. For example, the computation required gradually builds from additive thinking, using addition and subtraction separately and together, to multiplicative thinking, where multiplication and division are connected conceptions. More complex interactions of these operations build up over the series as the operations are used to both come to terms with problems' meanings and to achieve solutions. Similarly, two-dimensional geometry is used at first but extended to more complex uses over the range of problems, then joined by interaction with three-dimensional ideas. Measurement, including chance and data, also extends over the series from length to perimeter, and from area to surface area and volume, drawing on the relationships among these concepts to organise solutions as well as give an understanding of the metric system. Time concepts range from interpreting timetables using 12-hour and 24-hour clocks, while investigations related to mass rely on both the concept itself and practical measurements.

The language in which the problems are expressed is relatively straightforward, although this too increases in complexity and length of expression across the books in terms of both the context in which the problems are set and the mathematical content that is required. It will always be a challenge for some pupils to 'unpack' the meaning from a worded problem, particularly as the problems' context, information and meanings expand. This ability is fundamental to the nature of mathematical problem-solving and needs to be built up with time and experiences rather than be diminished or left out of the problems' situations. One reason for the suggestion that pupils work in groups is to allow them to share and assist each other with the tasks of discerning meanings and ways to tackle the ideas in complex problems through discussion, rather than simply leaping into the first ideas that come to mind (leaving the full extent of the problem unrealised).

An approach to solving problems

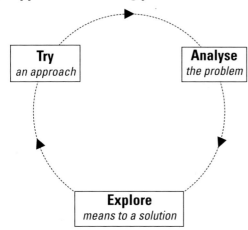

The careful, gradual development of an ability to analyse problems for meaning, organising information to make it meaningful and to make the connections among the problems more meaningful in order to suggest a way forward to a solution is fundamental to the approach taken with this series, from the first book to the last. At first, materials are used explicitly to aid these meanings and connections; however, in time they give way to diagrams, tables and symbols as understanding and experience of solving complex, engaging problems increases. As the problem forms expand, the range of methods to solve problems is carefully extended, not only to allow pupils to

successfully solve the many types of problems, but also to give them a repertoire of solution processes that they can consider and draw on when new situations are encountered. In turn, this allows them to explore one or another of these approaches to see whether each might furnish a likely result. In this way, when they try a particular method to solve a new problem, experience and analysis of the particular situation assists them in developing a full solution.

Not only is this model for the problem-solving process helpful in solving problems, it also provides a basis for pupils to discuss their progress and solutions and determine whether or not they have fully answered a question. At the same time, it guides teachers' questions of pupils and provides a means of seeing underlying mathematical difficulties and ways in which problems can be adapted to suit particular needs and extensions. Above all, it provides a common framework for discussions between a teacher and group or whole class to focus on the problem-solving process rather than simply on the solution of particular problems. Indeed, as Alan Schoenfeld, in Steen L. (Ed) *Mathematics and democracy* (2001), states so well, in problem-solving:

getting the answer is only the beginning rather than the end ... an ability to communicate thinking is equally important.

We wish all teachers and pupils who use these books success in fostering engagement with problem-solving and building a greater capacity to come to terms with and solve mathematical problems at all levels.

George Booker and Denise Bond

CONTENTS

Problem-solving and mathematical thinking

> *By learning problem-solving in mathematics, pupils should acquire ways of thinking, habits of persistence and curiosity, and confidence in unfamiliar situations that will serve them well outside the mathematics classroom. In everyday life and in the workplace, being a good problem solver can lead to great advantages.*
>
> **NCTM-Principles and standards for school mathematics (2000, p. 52)**

Problem-solving lies at the heart of mathematics. New mathematical concepts and processes have always grown out of problem situations and pupils' problem-solving capabilities develop from the very beginning of mathematics learning. A need to solve a problem can motivate pupils to acquire new ways of thinking as well as come to terms with concepts and processes that might not have been adequately learned when first introduced. Even those who can calculate efficiently and accurately are ill prepared for a world where new and adaptable ways of thinking are essential if they are unable to identify which information or processes are needed.

On the other hand, pupils who can analyse the meaning of problems, explore means to a solution and carry out a plan to solve mathematical problems have acquired deeper and more useful knowledge than simply being able to complete calculations, name shapes, use formulas to make measurements or determine measures of chance and data. It is critical that mathematics teaching focuses on enabling all pupils to become both able and willing to engage with and solve mathematical problems.

Well-chosen problems encourage deeper exploration of mathematical ideas, build persistence and highlight the need to understand thinking strategies, properties and relationships. They also reveal the central role of *sense making* in mathematical thinking—not only to evaluate the need for assessing the reasonableness of an answer or solution, but also the need to consider the interrelationships among the information provided with a problem situation. This may take the form of number sense, allowing numbers to be represented in various ways and operations to be interconnected; through spatial sense that allows the visualisation of a problem in both its parts and whole; to a sense of measurement across length, area, volume and chance and data.

Problem-solving

A problem is a task or situation for which there is no immediate or obvious solution, so that *problem-solving* refers to the processes used when engaging with this task. When problem-solving, pupils engage with situations for which a solution strategy is not immediately obvious, drawing on their understanding of concepts and processes they have already met, and will often develop new understandings and ways of thinking as they move towards a solution. It follows that a task that is a problem for one pupil may not be a problem for another and that a situation that is a problem at one level will only be an exercise or routine application of a known means to a solution at a later time.

For a pupil aged 5–6 years, sorting out the information about being on the lily pad and being in the water may take some consideration and require counters to represent the numbers and find the answer. For children in the middle primary years, understanding of the addition concept and knowledge of the addition facts would lead them immediately to think about the sum of 3 and 4 and come up with the solution of 7 frogs.

As the world in which we live becomes ever more complex, the level of mathematical thinking and problem-solving needed in life and in the workplace has increased considerably. Those who understand and can use the mathematics they have learned will have opportunities opened to them that those who do not develop these ways of thinking will not. To enable pupils to thrive in this changing world, attitudes and ways of knowing that enable them to deal with new or unfamiliar tasks are now as essential as the procedures that have always been used to handle familiar operations readily and efficiently. Such an attitude needs to develop from the beginning of mathematics learning as pupils form beliefs about meaning, the notion of taking control over the activities they engage with and the results they obtain, and as they build an inclination to try different approaches. In other words, pupils need to see mathematics as a way of thinking rather than a means of providing answers to be judged right or wrong by a teacher, textbook or some other external authority. They must be led to focus on means of solving problems rather than on particular answers so that they understand the need to determine the meaning of a problem before beginning to work on a solution.

In a car race, Jordan started in fourth place. During the race, he was passed by six cars. How many cars does he need to pass to win the race?

In order to solve this problem, it is not enough to simply use the numbers that are given. Rather, an analysis of the race situation is needed first to see

that when Jordan started, there were 3 cars ahead of him. When another 6 cars passed him, there were now 9 ahead of him. If he is to win, he needs to pass all 9 cars. The 4 and 6 implied in the problem were not used at all! Rather, a diagram or the use of materials is needed first to interpret the situation and then see how a solution can be obtained.

However, many pupils feel inadequate when they encounter problem-solving questions. They seem to have no idea of how to go about finding a solution and are unable to draw on the competencies they have learned in number, space and measurement. Often these difficulties stem from underdeveloped concepts for the operations, spatial thinking and measurement processes. They may also involve an underdeveloped capacity to read problems for meaning and a tendency to be led astray by the wording or numbers in a problem situation. Their approach may then simply be to try a series of guesses or calculations rather than consider using a diagram or materials to come to terms with what the problem is asking and using a systematic approach to organise the information given and required in the task. It is this ability to analyse problems that is the key to problem-solving, enabling decisions to be made about which mathematical processes to use, which information is needed and which ways of proceeding are likely to lead to a solution.

Making sense in mathematics

Making sense of the mathematics being developed and used must be seen as the central concern of learning. This is important, not only in coming to terms with problems and means to solutions, but also in terms of bringing meaning, representations and relationships in mathematical ideas to the forefront of thinking about and dealing with mathematics. Making sensible interpretations of any results and determining which of several possibilities is more or equally likely is critical in problem-solving.

Number sense, which involves being able to work with numbers comfortably and competently, is important in many aspects of problem-solving, in making judgments, interpreting information and communicating ways of thinking. It is based on a full understanding of numeration concepts such as zero, place value and the renaming of numbers in equivalent forms, so that 207 can be seen as 20 tens and 7 ones as well as 2 hundreds and 7 ones (or that $\frac{5}{2}$, 2.5 and $2\frac{1}{2}$ are all names for the same fraction amount). Automatic, accurate access to basic facts also underpins number sense, not as an end in itself, but rather as a means of combining with numeration concepts to allow manageable mental strategies and fluent processes for larger numbers. Well-understood concepts for the operations are essential in allowing relationships within a problem to be revealed and taken into account when framing a solution.

Number sense requires:

- understanding relationships among numbers
- appreciating the relative size of numbers
- a capacity to calculate and estimate mentally
- fluent processes for larger numbers and adaptive use of calculators
- an inclination to use understanding and facility with numeration and computation in flexible ways.

The following problem highlights the importance of these understandings.

There were 317 people at the New Year's Eve party on 31 December. If each table could seat 5 couples, how many tables were needed?

Reading the problem carefully shows that each table seats five couples or 10 people. At first glance, this problem might be solved using division; however, this would result in a decimal fraction, which is not useful in dealing with people seated at tables:

$$10\overline{)317} \text{ is } 31.7$$

In contrast, a full understanding of numbers allows 317 to be renamed as 31 tens and 7 ones:

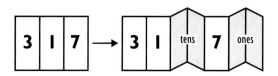

This provides for all the people at the party and analysis of the number 317 shows that there have to be at least 32 tables for everyone to have a seat and allow partygoers to move around and sit with others during the evening. Understanding how to *rename* a number has provided a direct solution without any need for computation. It highlights how coming to terms with a problem and integrating this with number sense provides a means of solving the problem more directly and allows an appreciation of what the solution might mean.

Spatial sense is equally important, as information is frequently presented in visual formats that need to be interpreted and processed, while the use of diagrams is often essential in developing conceptual understanding across all aspects of mathematics. Using diagrams, placing information in tables or depicting a systematic way of dealing with the various possibilities in a problem assist in visualising what is happening. It can be a very powerful tool in coming to terms with the information in a problem, and it provides insight into ways to proceed to a solution.

Spatial sense involves:

- a capacity to visualise shapes and their properties
- determining relationships among shapes and their properties
- linking two-dimensional and three-dimensional representations
- presenting and interpreting information in tables and lists
- an inclination to use diagrams and models to visualise problem situations and applications in flexible ways.

The following problem shows how these understandings can be used.

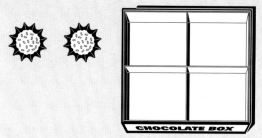

Cathy has 2 chocolates and 1 box. In how many different ways can she place the chocolates in the box?

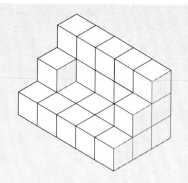

How many cubes are needed to make this shape?

Reading the problem carefully shows that only two spaces in the box can be used each time and that no use of the spaces can be duplicated. A systematic approach, placing one chocolate in a fixed position and varying the other spaces will provide a solution; however, care will be needed to see that the same placement has not already occurred:

There are six possible arrangements. The placement of objects on the diagram has provided a solution, highlighting how coming to terms with a problem and integrating this with spatial sense allows a systematic analysis of all the possibilities.

Similar thinking is used with arrangements of two-dimensional and three-dimensional shapes and in visualising how they can fit together or be taken apart.

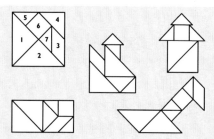

Which of these shapes can be made using all of the tangram pieces?

Measurement sense is dependent on both number sense and spatial sense, since attributes that are one-, two- or three-dimensional are quantified to provide both exact and approximate measures and allow comparison. Many measurements use aspects of space (length, area, volume), while others use numbers on a scale (time, mass, temperature). Money can be viewed as a measure of value and uses numbers more directly, while practical activities such as map reading and determining angles require a sense of direction as well as gauging measurement. The coordination of the thinking for number and space, along with an understanding of how the metric system builds on place value, zero and renaming, is critical in both building measurement understanding and using it to come to terms with and solve many practical problems and applications.

Measurement sense includes:

- understanding how numeration and computation underpin measurement
- extending relationships from number understanding to the metric system
- appreciating the relative size of measurements
- a capacity to use calculators, mental or written processes for exact and approximate calculations
- an inclination to use understanding and facility with measurements in flexible ways.

The following problem shows how these understandings can be used.

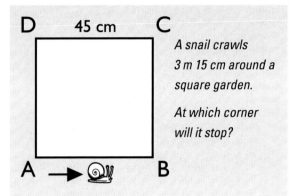

A snail crawls 3 m 15 cm around a square garden.

At which corner will it stop?

Carefully reading the problem shows that the snail will travel 45 cm as it moves along each side of the square. In order to come to terms with what is needed, 3 m 15 cm needs to be renamed as 315 cm. The distances the snail travels along each side can then be totalled until 315 cm is reached. It can also be inferred that it will travel along some sides more than once as the distance around the outside of the square is 180 cm. At this point, the snail will be back at A. Travelling a further 45 cm will take it to B, a distance of 225 cm. At C it will have travelled 270 cm and it will have travelled 315 cm (or 3 m 15 cm) when it reaches D for the second time.

By using an understanding of the problem situation, a diagram has been integrated with the knowledge of metres and centimetres and a capacity to calculate mentally using addition and multiplication to provide an appropriate solution. Both spatial sense and number sense have been used to understand the problem and suggest a means to a solution.

Data sense is an outgrowth of measurement sense and refers to an understanding of the way number sense, spatial sense and a sense of measurement work together to deal with situations where patterns need to be discerned among data or when likely outcomes need to be analysed. This can occur among frequencies in data or possibilities in chance.

Data sense involves:

- understanding how numeration and computation underpin the analysis of data
- appreciating the relative likelihood of outcomes
- a capacity to use calculators or mental and written processes for exact and approximate calculations
- presenting and interpreting data in tables and graphs
- an inclination to use understanding and facility with number combinations and arrangements in flexible ways.

The following problem shows how these understandings can be used.

You are allowed 3 scoops of ice-cream: 1 chocolate, 1 vanilla and 1 strawberry. How many different ways can the scoops be placed on a cone?

There are six possibilities for placing the scoops of ice-cream on a cone. Systematically treating the possible placements one at a time highlights how the use of a diagram can account for all possible arrangements.

This problem also shows how *patterning* is another aspect of sense-making in mathematics. Often a problem calls on discerning a pattern in the placement of materials, the numbers involved in the situation or the possible arrangements of data or outcomes to determine a likely solution. Being able to see patterns is also very helpful in getting an immediate solution or understanding whether or not a solution is complete. Allied to patterning are notions of symmetry, repetition and extending ideas to more general cases. All of these aspects of mathematical sense-making are critical to developing the thinking on which problem-solving depends, as well as solving problems per se.

As more experience in solving problems is gained, an ability to see patterns in what is occurring will also allow solutions to be obtained more directly and help in seeing the relationship between a new problem and one that has been solved previously. It is this ability to relate problem types, even when the context appears to be quite different, that often distinguishes a good problem solver from one who is more hesitant.

Building a problem-solving process

While the teaching of problem-solving has often centred on the use of particular strategies that could apply to various classes of problems, many pupils are unable to access and use these strategies to solve problems outside of the teaching situations in which they were introduced. Rather than acquire a process for solving problems, they may attempt to memorise a set of procedures and view mathematics as a set of learned rules where success follows the use of the right procedure to the numbers given in the problem. Any use of strategies may be based on familiarity, personal preference or recent exposure rather than through a consideration of the problem to be solved. A pupil may even feel it is sufficient to have only one strategy and that the strategy should work all of the time—and if it doesn't, then the problem can't be solved.

In contrast, observation of successful problem-solvers shows that their success depends more on an analysis of the problem itself—what is being asked, what information might be used, what answer might be likely and so on—so that a particular approach is used only after the intent of the problem is determined. Establishing the meaning of the problem before any plan is drawn up or work on a solution begins is critical. Pupils need to see that discussion about the problem's meaning, and the ways of obtaining a solution, must take precedence over a focus on the answer. Using collaborative groups when problem-solving, rather than tasks assigned individually, is an approach that helps to develop this disposition.

Looking at a problem and working through what is needed to solve it will shed light on the problem-solving process.

On Saturday, Peta went to the shopping centre to buy a new outfit to wear at her friend's birthday party. She spent half of her money on a dress and then one-third of what she had left on a pair of sandals. After her purchases, she had £60.00 left in her purse. How much money did she have to start with?

By reading the problem carefully, it can be determined that Peta had an original amount of money to spend. She spent some on a dress and some on shoes and then had £60.00 left. All of the information required to solve the problem is available and no further information is needed. The question at the end asks how much money did she start with, but really the problem is how much did she spend on the dress and then on the sandals.

The discussion of this problem has served to identify the key element within the problem-solving process; it is necessary to analyse the problem to unfold its meanings and discover what needs to be considered. What the problem is asking is rarely found in the question in the problem statement. Instead, it is necessary to look below the surface level of the problem and come to terms with the problem's structure. Reading the problem aloud, thinking of previous problems and other similar problems, selecting important information from the problem that may be useful, and discussion of the problem's meaning are all essential.

The next step is to explore possible ways to solve the problem. If the analysis stage has been completed, then ways in which the problem might be solved will emerge.

It is here that strategies, and how they might be useful to solving a problem, can arise. However, most problems can be solved in a variety of ways, using different approaches, and pupils need to be encouraged to select a method that makes sense and appears achievable.

Ways that may come to mind during the analysis include:

- *Materials* – Base 10 materials could be used to represent the money spent and to help the pupil work backwards through the problem from when Peta had £60.00 left.

- *Try and adjust* – Select an amount that Peta might have taken shopping, try it in the context of the question, examine the resulting amounts, and then adjust them, if necessary, until £60.00 is the result.

- *Backtrack using the numbers* – The sandals were one-third of what was left after the dress, so the £60.00 would be two-thirds of what was left. Together, these two amounts would match the cost of the dress.

- *Use a diagram* to represent the information in the problem.

- *Think of a similar problem* – For example, it is like the car race problem in that the relative portions (places) are known and the final result (money left, winning position) are given.

Now *one* of the possible means to a solution can be selected to try. Backtracking shows that £60 was two-thirds of what she had left, so the sandals (which are one-third of what she had left) must have cost £30. Together, these are half of what Peta took, which is also the cost of the dress. As the dress cost £90, Peta took £180 to spend.

Materials could also have been used with which to work backwards: 6 tens represent the £60 left, so the sandals would cost 3 tens and the dress 9 tens—she took 18 tens or £180 shopping.

Another way to solve the problem is with a diagram. If we use a rectangle to represent how much money Peta took with her, we can show by shading how much she spent on a dress and sandals:

Total amount available to spend:

She spent half of her money on a dress.

She then spent one-third of what she had left on sandals, which has minimised and simplified the calculations.

At this point she had £60 left, so the two unshaded parts must be worth £60 or £30 per part—which has again minimised and simplified the calculations.

	£30	£30

Each of the six equal parts represents £30, so Peta took £180 to spend.

Having tried an idea, an answer needs to be analysed in the light of the problem in case another solution is required. It is essential to compare an answer to the original analysis of the problem to determine whether the solution obtained is reasonable and answers the problem. It will also raise the question as to whether other answers exist and even whether there might be other solution strategies. In this way the process is cyclic and should the answer be unreasonable, then the process would need to begin again.

We believe that Peta took £180 to shop with. She spent half (or £90) on a dress, leaving £90. She spent one-third of the £90 on sandals (£30), leaving £60. Looking again at the problem, we see that this is correct and the diagram has provided a direct means to the solution that has minimised and simplified the calculations.

Thinking about the various ways this problem was solved highlights the key elements within the problem-solving process. When starting the process, it is necessary to *analyse* the problem to unfold its layers, discover its structure and understand what the problem is really asking. Next, all possible ways to solve the problem are *explored* before one, or a combination of ways, are selected to *try*. Finally, once something is tried, it is important to check the solution in relation to the problem to see if the solution is reasonable. This process highlights the cyclic nature of problem-solving and brings to the fore the importance of understanding the problem (and its structure) before proceeding. This process can be summarised as:

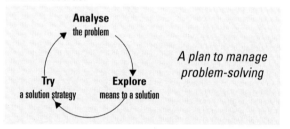

A plan to manage problem-solving

This model for problem-solving provides pupils with a means of talking about the steps they take whenever they have a problem to solve: Discussing how they initially analysed the problem, explored various ways that might provide a solution, and then tried one or more possible solution paths to obtain a solution—which they then analysed for completeness and sense-making—reinforces the very methods that will give them success on future problems. This process brings to the fore the importance of understanding the problem and its structure before proceeding.

Further, returning to an analysis of any answers and solution strategies highlights the importance of reflecting on what has been done. Taking time to reflect on any plans drawn up, processes followed and strategies used brings out the significance of coming to terms with the nature of the problem, as well as the value and applicability of particular approaches that might be used with other problems. Thinking of how a related problem was solved is often the key to solving another problem at a later stage. It allows the

thinking to be carried over to the new situation in a way that simply trying to think of the strategy used often fails to reveal. Analysing problems in this way also highlights that a problem is not solved until the answer obtained can be justified. Learning to reflect on the *whole* process leads to the development of a deeper understanding of problem-solving, and time must be allowed for reflection and discussion to fully build mathematical thinking.

Managing a problem-solving programme

Teaching problem-solving differs from many other aspects of mathematics in that collaborative work can be more productive than individual work. Pupils who may be tempted to quickly give up when working on their own can be encouraged to see ways of proceeding when discussing a problem in a group; therefore building greater confidence in their capacity to solve problems and learning the value of persisting with a problem in order to tease out what is required. What is discussed with their peers is more likely to be recalled when other problems are met, while the observations made in the group increase the range of approaches that a pupil can access. Thus, time has to be allowed for discussion and exploration rather than insisting that pupils spend 'time on task' as for routine activities.

Correct answers that fully solve a problem are always important, but developing a capacity to use an effective problem-solving process needs to be the highest priority. A pupil who has an answer should be encouraged to discuss his or her solution with others who believe they have a solution, rather than tell his or her answer to another pupil or simply move on to another problem. In particular, explaining to others why he or she believes an answer is reasonable, as well as why it provides a solution, gets other pupils to focus on the entire problem-solving process rather than just quickly getting an answer.

Expressing an answer in a sentence that relates to the question stated in the problem also encourages reflection on what was done and ensures that the focus is on solving the problem rather than providing an answer. These aspects of the teaching of problem-solving should then be taken further, as particular groups discuss their solutions with the whole class and all pupils are able to participate in the discussion of the problem. In this way, problem-solving as a way of thinking comes to the fore, rather than focusing on the answers as the main aim of their mathematical activities.

Questions must encourage pupils to explore possible means to a solution and try one or more of them, rather than point to a particular procedure. It can also help pupils to see how to progress in their thinking, rather than get into a loop where the same steps are repeated over and over. While having too many questions that focus on the way to a solution may end up removing the problem-solving aspect from the question, having too few may cause pupils to become frustrated with the task and think that it is beyond them. Pupils need to experience the challenge of problem-solving and gain pleasure from working through the process that leads to a full solution. Taking time to listen to pupils as they try out their ideas, without comment or without directing them to a particular strategy, is also important. Listening provides a sense of how pupils' problem-solving is developing, as assessing this aspect of mathematics can be difficult. After all, solving one problem will not necessarily lead to success on the next problem, nor will difficulty with a particular problem mean that the problems that follow will also be as challenging.

A teacher also may need to extend or adapt a given problem to ensure the problem-solving process is understood and can be used in other situations, instead of moving on to a different problem in another area of mathematics learning. This can help pupils to understand the significance of asking questions of a problem, as well as seeing how a way of thinking can be adapted to other related problems. Having pupils engage in this process of problem posing is another way of both assessing them and bringing them to terms with the overall process of solving problems.

Building a problem-solving process

The cyclical model *Analyse–Explore–Try* provides a very helpful means of organising and discussing possible solutions. However, care must be taken that it is not seen simply as a procedure to be memorised and then applied in a routine manner to every new problem. Rather, it needs to be carefully developed over a range of different problems, highlighting the components that are developed with each new problem.

Analyse

- As pupils read a problem, the need to first read for the *meaning* of the problem can be stressed. This may require reading more than once and can be helped by asking pupils to state in their own words what the problem is asking them to do.

- Further reading will be needed to sort out which information is needed and whether some is not needed or if other information needs to be gathered from the problem's context (e.g. data presented within the illustration or table accompanying the problem), or whether the pupils' mathematical understandings need to be used to find other relationships among the information. As the form of the problems becomes more complex, this thinking will be extended to incorporate further ways of dealing with the information; for example, measurement units, fractions and larger numbers might need to be renamed to the same mathematical form.

- Thinking about any processes that might be needed and the order in which they are used, as well as the type of answer that could occur, should also be developed in the context of new levels of problem structure.

- Developing a capacity to see 'through' the problem's expression—or context to see similarities between new problems and others that might already have been met—is a critical way of building expertise in coming to terms with and solving problems.

Explore

- When a problem is being explored, some problems will require the use of materials to think through the whole of the problem's context. Others will demand the use of diagrams to show what is needed. Another will show how systematic analysis of the situation using a sequence of diagrams, on a list or table, is helpful. As these ways of thinking about the problem are understood, they can be included in the cycle of steps.

Try

- Many pupils often try to guess a result. This can even be encouraged by talking about 'guess and check' as a means to solve problems. Changing to 'try and adjust' is more helpful in building a way of thinking and can lead to a very powerful way of finding solutions.

Expanding the problem-solving process

- Put the solution back into the problem.
- Does the answer make sense?
- Does it solve the problem?
- Is it the only answer?
- Could there be another way?

- Read carefully.
- What is the problem asking?
- What is the meaning of the information? Is it all needed? Is there too little? Too much?
- Which operations will be needed and in what order?
- What sort of answer is likely?
- Have I seen a problem like this before?

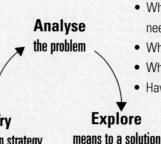

Analyse the problem

Try a solution strategy

Explore means to a solution

- Use materials or a model.
- Use a calculator.
- Use pencil and paper.
- Look for a pattern.

- Use a diagram or materials.
- Work backwards or backtrack.
- Put the information into a table.
- Try and adjust.

- When materials, a diagram or table have been used, another means to a solution is to look for a pattern in the results. When these have revealed what is needed to try for a solution, it may also be reasonable to use pencil and paper or a calculator.

Analyse

- The point in the cycle where an answer is assessed for reasonableness (e.g. whether it provides a solution, is only one of several solutions or whether there may be another way to solve the problem) also needs to be brought to the fore as different problems are met.

The role of calculators

When calculators are used, pupils devote less time to basic calculations, providing time that might be needed to either explore a solution or find an answer to a problem. In this way, attention is shifted from computation, which the calculator can do, to thinking about the problem and its solution—work that the calculator cannot do. It also allows more problems (and more realistic problems) to be addressed in problem-solving sessions. In these situations, a calculator serves as a tool rather than a crutch, requiring pupils to think through the problem's solution in order to know how to use the calculator appropriately. It also underpins the need to make sense of the steps along the way and any answers that result, as keying incorrect numbers, operations or order of operations quickly leads to results that are not appropriate.

Choosing, adapting and extending problems

When problems are selected, they need to be examined to see if pupils already have an understanding of the underlying mathematics required and that the problem's expression can be meaningfully read by the group of pupils who will be attempting the solution—though not necessarily by *all* pupils in the group. The problem itself should be neither too easy (so that it is just an exercise, repeating something readily done before), nor too difficult (thus beyond the capabilities of most or all in the group). A problem should engage the interests of the pupils and also be able to be solved in more than one way.

As a problem and its solution is reviewed, posing similar questions—where the numbers, shapes or measurements are changed—focuses attention back on what was entailed in analysing the problem and in exploring the means to a solution. Extending these processes to more complex situations shows how the particular approach can be extended to other situations and how patterns can be analysed to obtain more general methods or results. It also highlights the importance of a systematic approach when conceiving and discussing a solution and can lead to pupils asking themselves further questions about the situation and pose problems of their own as the significance of the problem's structure is uncovered.

Problem structure and expression

When analysing a problem, it is also possible to discern critical aspects of the problem's form and relate this to an appropriate level of mathematics and problem expression when choosing or extending problems. A problem of first-level complexity uses simple mathematics and simple language. A second-level problem may have simple language and more difficult mathematics or more difficult language and simple mathematics, while a third-level problem has yet more difficult language and mathematics. Within a problem, the processes that must be used may be more or less obvious, the information that is required for a solution may be too much or too little, and strategic thinking may be needed in order to come to terms with what the problem is asking.

Level	processes obvious	processes less obvious	too much information	too little information	strategic thinking
increasing difficulty with problem's expression and mathematics required	simple expression, simple mathematics				
	more complex expression, simple mathematics				
	simple expression, more complex mathematics				
	complex expression, complex mathematics				

The varying levels of problem structure and expression

(i) The processes to be used are relatively obvious, as these problems are comparatively straightforward and contain all the information necessary to find a solution.

(ii) The processes required are not immediately obvious, as these problems contain all the information necessary to find a solution but demand further analysis to sort out what is wanted and pupils may need to reverse what initially seemed to be required.

(iii) The problem contains more information than is needed for a solution, as these problems contain not only all the information needed to find a solution but also additional information in the form of times, numbers, shapes or measurements.

(iv) Further information must be gathered and applied to the problem in order to obtain a solution. These problems do not contain all the information necessary to find a solution but do contain a means to obtain the required information. The problem's setting, the pupil's mathematical understanding or the problem's wording need to be searched for the additional material.

(v) Strategic thinking is required to analyse the question in order to determine a solution strategy. Deeper analysis, often aided by the use of diagrams or tables, is needed to come to terms with what the problem is asking so a means to a solution can be determined.

This analysis of the nature of problems can also serve as a means of evaluating the provision of problems within a mathematics programme. In particular, it can lead to the development of a full range of problems, ensuring they are included across all problem forms, with the mathematics and expression suited to the level of the pupils.

Assessing problem-solving

Assessment of problem-solving requires careful and close observation of pupils working in a problem-solving setting. These observations can reveal the range of problem forms and the level of complexity in the expression and underlying mathematics that a pupil is able to confidently deal with. Further analysis of these observations can show to what extent the pupil is able to analyse the question, explore ways to a solution, select one or more methods to try and then analyse any results obtained. It is the combination of two fundamental aspects—the types of problem that can be solved and the manner in which solutions are carried out—that will give a measure of a pupil's developing problem-solving abilities, rather than a one-off test in which some problems are solved and others are not.

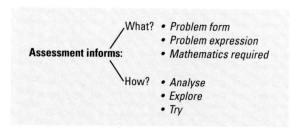

Observations based on this analysis have led to a categorisation of many of the possible difficulties that pupils experience with problem-solving as a whole, rather than the misconceptions they may have about particular problems. These often involve inappropriate attempts at a solution based on little understanding of the problem.

A major cause of possible difficulties is the *lack of a well-developed plan* of attack, leading pupils to focus on the *surface level* of problems. In such cases, pupils:

- locate and manipulate numbers with little or no thought about their relevance to the problem
- try a succession of different operations if the first ones attempted do not yield a (likely) result
- focus on keywords for an indication of what might be done without considering their significance within the problem as a whole
- read problems quickly and cursorily to locate the numbers to be used

Problem	Likely causes
Pupil is unable to make any attempt at a solution.	• not interested • feels overwhelmed • cannot think of how to start to answer question • needs to reconsider complexity of steps and information
Pupil has no means of linking the situation to the implicit mathematical meaning.	• needs to create diagram or use materials • needs to consider separate parts of question and then bring parts together
Pupil uses an inappropriate operation.	• misled by word cues or numbers • has underdeveloped concepts • uses rote procedures rather than real understanding
Pupil is unable to translate a problem into a more familiar process.	• cannot see interactions between operations • lack of understanding means he/she unable to reverse situations • data may need to be used in an order not evident in the problem statement or in an order contrary to that in which it is presented

• use the first available word cue to suggest the operation that might be needed.

Other possible difficulties result from a focus on being quick, which leads to:

• no attempt to assess the reasonableness of an answer

• little perseverance if an answer is not obtained using the first approach tried

• not being able to access strategies to which they have been introduced.

When the approaches to problem processing developed in this series are followed and the specific suggestions for solving particular problems or types of problems are discussed with pupils, these difficulties can be minimised, if not entirely avoided. Analysing the problem before starting leads to an understanding of the problem's meanings. The cycle of steps within the model means that nothing is tried before the intent of the problem is clear and the means to a solution have been considered. Focusing on a problem's meaning and discussing what needs to be done builds perseverance. Making sense of the steps that must be followed and any answers that result are central to the problem-solving process. These difficulties are unlikely to occur among those who have built up an understanding of this way of thinking.

A final comment

If an approach to problem-solving can be built up using the ideas developed here and the problems in the investigations on the pages that follow, pupils will develop a way of thinking about and with mathematics that will allow them to readily solve problems and generalise from what they already know to understand new mathematical ideas. They will engage with these emerging mathematical conceptions from their very beginnings, be prepared to debate and discuss their own ideas, and develop attitudes that will allow them to tackle new problems and topics. Mathematics can then be a subject that is readily engaged with and can become one in which the pupil feels in control, instead of one in which many rules devoid of meaning have to be memorised and applied at the right time. This early enthusiasm for learning and the ability to think mathematically will lead to a search for meaning in new situations and processes that will allow mathematical ideas to be used across a range of applications in school and everyday life.

Problem-solving
To reason logically and to identify, create and describe patterns.

Curriculum links
England (Year 2)
- Using and applying: Describe patterns and relationships.

Northern Ireland (Key Stage 1)
- Processes in maths: Develop different approaches to problem solving.
- Processes in maths: Recognise simple patterns and relationships.

Scotland (First)
- Patterns and relationships: Continue and devise repeating patterns.

Wales (Foundation)
- Skills: Develop a variety of mathematical approaches and strategies.
- Skills: Recognise patterns through practical activities.

Materials
Blocks such as Unifix™ cubes or counters (for example, teddies or plastic animals) in four different colours

Focus
These pages explore making patterns, changing patterns and using patterns and numbers. Pupils analyse what makes a pattern and make predictions based on their experiences.

Discussion
Page 3
The first activity involves taking four blocks (of different colours) and lining them up in different groups of two. It is important to explain to pupils that there can be two groups with the same two colours but they have to be lined up in a different order. The possible arrangements are:

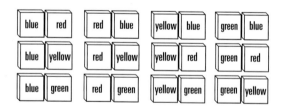

The same concept is extended in the next activity, where pupils now line up the blocks in groups of three. For example, a pupil might keep the same colour first and then change the next two colours or he/she might change the first colour and then swap the following two colours. Encourage pupils to explore different ways and arrangements. The possible arrangements are:

red blue green	red yellow blue	blue red green
red blue yellow	red yellow green	blue red yellow
red green yellow	blue green red	blue yellow green
red green blue	blue green yellow	blue yellow red
green blue red	green yellow red	yellow blue green
green blue yellow	green yellow blue	yellow blue red
green red blue	yellow red blue	yellow green red
green red yellow	yellow red green	yellow green blue

Page 4
This activity builds on the previous experience of lining up the blocks and interchanging the colours to make the pattern. The grid can be organised in a number of ways; however, each different way will always have the same diagonal with three blocks of the same colour. Two grids are provided to enable pupils to explore and try different possible arrangements.

Page 5
This activity builds on and extends the previous experience of the three-by-three grid by extending the grid to four-by-four with an additional colour. Again, the grid can be organised in a number of ways and this time it is possible for both diagonals to have four blocks of the same colour. Two grids are provided to enable pupils to explore and try different possible arrangements.

Possible difficulties
- Indiscriminately moving blocks around
- Unable to keep track of what has already been tried
- Content to find only one possibility
- Unable to consider both rows and columns

Extension
- Pupils can be encouraged to make and describe more complex patterns of their own.
- Extend the grid to five-by-five, using five different colours.

BLOCKS

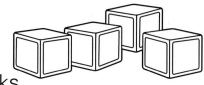

Take 4 blocks, each a different colour;
for example: red, blue, green and yellow.

1. Line up and draw different groups of 2 blocks.

2. How many different groups can you make? _____

3. Now, line up and draw different groups of 3 blocks.

4. How many can you make? _____

Make 3 groups of 3 blocks (9 blocks), with each group a different colour.

Place the blocks on the grid, making sure that no row or column has the same colour in it more than once.

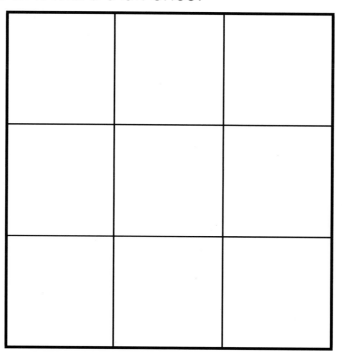

What do you notice about the diagonals? _____

_____

Try doing it a different way.

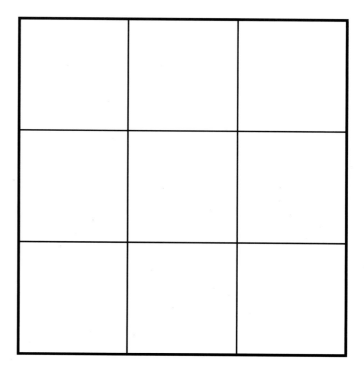

MORE BLOCKS

Make 4 groups of 4 blocks (16 blocks), with each group a different colour.

Place the blocks on the grid, making sure that no row or column has the same colour in it more than once.

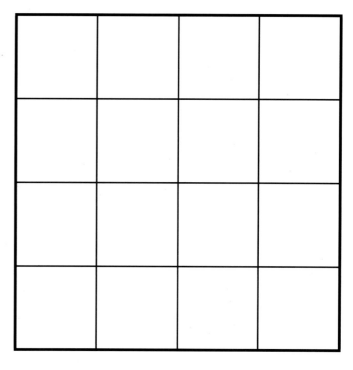

What pattern do you notice? _____

_____

Try doing it a different way.

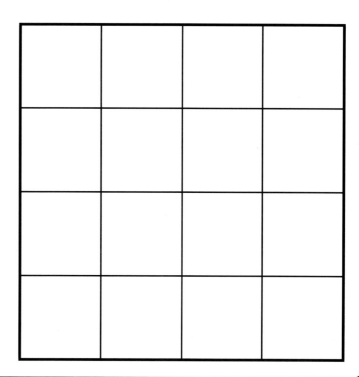

Problem-solving

To reason logically and to use patterns to represent and solve problems.

Curriculum links

England (Year 2)
- Using and applying: Describe patterns and relationships.

Northern Ireland (Key Stage 1)
- Processes in maths: Develop different approaches to problem solving.
- Processes in maths: Recognise simple patterns and relationships.

Scotland (First)
- Patterns and relationships: Continue and devise repeating patterns.

Wales (Foundation)
- Skills: Develop a variety of mathematical approaches and strategies.
- Skills: Recognise patterns through practical activities.

Materials

Blocks such as Unifix™ cubes or counters (For each group, 16 in total: 6 red, 3 blue, 5 green and 2 yellow.)

Focus

These pages explore analysing problems with a three-dimensional aspect. They build on and extend the previous work with coloured blocks on page 3. There are various solutions to this problem and pupils should be encouraged to explore and try a number of different possibilities.

Discussion

Page 7

Individually or in pairs, pupils use the 16 blocks and place them on their street according to the street map; for example: the 6 red people could be 1 apartment block and 3 houses; 1 apartment block, 1 house and 1 townhouse; or 2 apartment blocks. However, the yellow blocks can only be 2 houses or 1 townhouse. Possible arrangements (using the red blocks) could be:

RED PEOPLE

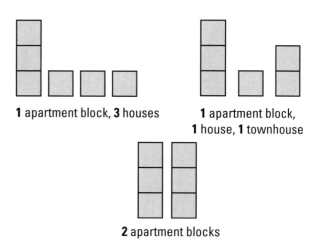

1 apartment block, **3** houses   **1** apartment block, **1** house, **1** townhouse

2 apartment blocks

Possible difficulties

- Pupils are making houses only
- When making apartments, colours are mixed
- Not realising that organising the blocks in a different order gives a different solution

Extension

- Using the 'Block Street' copymaster, make up other criteria for pupils to make streets.
- Take a digital photo of each Block Street and have the pairs write about their street, listing how many houses there are.

BLOCK STREET

Place blocks on the street to show:

house = **1** block

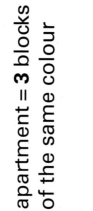

townhouse = **2** blocks
of the same colour

apartment = **3** blocks
of the same colour

16 people live in Block Street:
6 red people, **3** blue people, **5** green people and **2** yellow people.

1. Make your street, placing houses, townhouses and apartments to show where the people live.

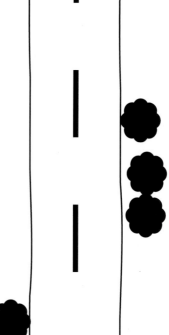

2. Using the same blocks, make a different-looking street.

Problem-solving

To identify and use information in a problem.

Curriculum links

England (Year 2)

- Using and applying: Solve problems in the context of numbers.
- Using and applying: Identify the information needed to solve a problem.

Northern Ireland (Key Stage 1)

- Processes in maths: Develop different approaches to problem solving.

Scotland (First)

- Addition: Use addition when solving problems.

Wales (Foundation)

- Skills: Develop a variety of mathematical approaches and strategies.

Focus

These pages explore the reading and interpreting of information to solve problems involving numeration (no addition or subtraction is needed to solve them). Pupils analyse the problem to locate the required information, decide which information is not needed and then use comparison rather than addition or subtraction to obtain solutions.

Discussion

Page 9

Anne skipped 10 more times than Maree, who skipped 42 times. In the next problem, pupils need to read what happened on Saturday and the next day to infer that the next day was Sunday. The last problem is about jelly beans, with the additional information (about marshmallows) not required. Although Aaron has the largest number, these are marshmallows and not jelly beans. Jane has the largest number of jelly beans.

Page 10

In the first problem, Julie has no (or zero) swap cards, so technically, she has the smallest number of cards. This can lead to a discussion about whether the problem means the smallest actual number or should include only the people who actually have cards. The next problem introduces the idea of organising information in a table to help find a solution. The question does not specify how many cards John lost or how many Carla won. The information in the table will show that John has the least number of cards and Carla the most. As John loses some cards, he still has the least number, while Carla winning some means she still has the most.

Page 11

This page introduces the concept of magic squares. Simple three-by-three magic squares have been used to enable pupils to come to terms with the idea that each row, column and diagonal adds to the magic number.

Possible difficulties

Pupils are unable to interpret the information in the problems, including:

- thinking that Maree skipped 42 times and Anna skipped only 10 times
- not being able to work out that the next day is Sunday
- not realising that having no cards means 0 (zero)
- not seeing that having the least number of cards and then losing more will always mean you will have the least cards, while having the most cards and winning more will mean you always have the most.

Inadequate numeration understanding

- Not understanding that zero, as a number, shows none of something.
- Counting or adding to find 10 more rather than using place value.
- Using comparison to determine least and greatest tens place value is not developed.

Extension

- Use a table to record information for the other problems and discuss how this helps in solving them.
- Investigate other magic squares.

Maree and Anne were skipping.
Maree skipped 42 times.
Anne skipped 10 more times.

1. Who skipped the most? _____

2. How many times did Maree skip? _____

On Saturday, Lee counted 46 ants and 23 caterpillars. The next day he counted 58 ants and 25 caterpillars.

3. How many ants did Lee count on Sunday?

_____

4. On which day did he count the most caterpillars?

_____

Jane had 32 jelly beans.
Aaron had 48 marshmallows.
Scott had 29 jelly beans.

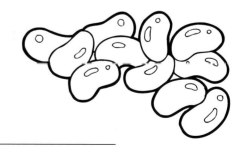

5. Who had the most jelly beans? _____

SWAP CARDS

Kerry has 42 swap cards.
Julie has no swap cards.
Valda has 35 swap cards.

1. Who has the smallest number of cards? _____

Mark has 53 swap cards.
John has 10 less than Mark.
Carla has 72 swap cards.

2. Use the table to record how many cards each person has.

Mark	John	Carla

The next day, John lost some cards and Carla won some cards.

3. Who has the most cards? _____

4. Who has the least cards? _____

2	7	6
9	5	1
4	3	8

In a magic square, every row, column and diagonal adds to the same number.

In this magic square all the rows, columns and diagonals add to **15**. Its magic number is **15**.

Look at the magic squares below. Remember, each row, column and diagonal must to add to the same number.

1. Figure out what the magic number of each square is.

2. Fill in the missing numbers in each square.

6		8
7	5	3
	9	

	1	6
3		7
		2

(a) Magic number: _____

(b) Magic number: _____

Problem-solving
To analyse and use information in addition problems.

Curriculum links
England (Year 2)
- Using and applying: Solve problems in the context of numbers.
- Using and applying: Identify and record the information or calculation needed to solve a problem.
- Knowing and using number facts: Derive and recall addition facts.
- Calculating: Add mentally.

Northern Ireland (Key Stage 1)
- Processes in maths: Select the mathematics appropriate for a task.
- Processes in maths: Develop different approaches to problem solving.
- Number: Understand the operation of addition and use addition facts.
- Number: Develop strategies for adding mentally.

Scotland (First)
- Addition: Use addition when solving problems.

Wales (Foundation)
- Skills: Develop a variety of mathematical approaches and strategies.
- Skills: Develop a variety of mental and written strategies of computation.
- Number: Calculate in a variety of ways.

Materials
Counters or blocks

Focus
These pages explore word problems that require addition. Pupils need to determine what the problem is asking in order to find a solution. Analysis of the problem reveals that different items may need to be added, which is more complex that just adding two or more of the same together. Other problems contain information that will not be needed.

Counters or blocks can be used to assist, since these problems are about reading for information and determining what the problem is asking, rather than just solving addition or basic fact problems.

Discussion
Page 13
The stories must be read first to see what information is needed. In the first three problems the word 'altogether' explicitly suggests addition. In the last problem, an understanding of the context is required to see that addition of the two numbers is needed.

Page 14
Some information (ordinal numbers, days of the week) is not needed to find a solution, while addition of several numbers is required. For the last problem, an understanding of the context shows that the numbers are added (despite the use of 'lost').

Page 15
Careful reading of the information in the stories is needed to sort out which numbers must be added. In the first problem, all the ducks must be added despite their different locations. In the other problems, analysing the question shows which information is to be used and which is to be discarded.

Possible difficulties
- Unable to identify that addition must be used to find a solution
- Confusion over the use of ordinal numbers and identifying which numbers must be added
- Adding all the numbers in a problem rather than identifying the additional information that is not needed
- Lack of ability to add readily and accurately

Extension
- Have pupils write problems for other pupils to complete. Use the problems on the page as a model.

IN THE GARDEN

1. In the garden, a caterpillar ate 23 leaves in the morning and 6 leaves in the afternoon. How many leaves did it eat altogether?

_____

2. There are 16 birds in the trees. 8 more fly in to join them. How many birds are there altogether?

_____

3. The farmer has 26 cows in one paddock and 39 cows in another paddock. How many cows are there altogether?

_____

4. Daniel picked 49 mangoes from one tree and 37 mangoes from another tree. How many mangoes does he have?

_____

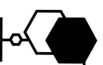

1. Amy went to the library. While there, she looked at 2 books on the first shelf, 4 books on the second shelf and 1 book on the third shelf. How many books did she look at?

_____

2. George went shopping for clothes. On the first floor he bought 5 shirts, on the second floor he bought 3 shirts, on the third floor he bought no shirts and on the fourth floor he bought 2 shirts. How many shirts did he buy?

_____

3. At the train station 19 people got into the first carriage, 17 people got into the second carriage and 12 people got into the third carriage. How many people got on the train?

_____

4. Claire's pet parrot has red, blue and green feathers. He lost 7 red feathers on Monday, 2 blue feathers on Tuesday and 5 red feathers on Wednesday. How many feathers did he lose?

_____

1. There were 23 ducks on the lake and 8 swans on the shore. 9 more ducks came to land on the lake. How many ducks were there altogether?

_____

2. There are 16 black goats by the river and 13 white goats eating grass. Another 7 black goats are under the trees. How many black goats are there?

_____

3. Matthew gave 6 guinea pigs to Class One. He also gave 5 budgies and 8 guinea pigs to Class Two. How many guinea pigs did he give away?

_____

4. There are 8 kangaroos sleeping under the gum trees and 5 koalas sleeping in the gum trees. Another 15 kangaroos are drinking at the water hole. How many kangaroos are there altogether?

_____

Problem-solving

To read, interpret and analyse information.

Curriculum links

England (Year 2)
- Using and applying: Solve problems in the context of numbers.
- Using and applying: Identify the information needed to solve a problem.
- Counting and understanding number: Explain what each digit in a two-digit number represents.

Northern Ireland (Key Stage 1)
- Processes in maths: Develop different approaches to problem solving.
- Number: Understand that the place of the digit indicates its value.

Scotland (First)
- Number processes: Know the link between a digit, its place and its value.

Wales (Foundation)
- Skills: Develop a variety of mathematical approaches and strategies.
- Number: Understand number and number notation.

Focus

This page explores relationships among numbers and uses this analysis to find a number that matches specific criteria. This process encourages pupils to first disregard numbers that are not possible rather than simply look for ones that are likely to work. Some pupils will use the listed information in order to discard numbers until only the correct number remains, while other pupils may prefer to try each number in turn against all of the criteria until they find a number that answers all conditions.

Discussion

Page 17

The criteria listed allow numbers to not only be selected but also to be ruled out; for example, *'more than 68'* rules out 20, 39 and 53. Having *'3 in the ones place'* means the number must be 73. Some pupils may work down the list of conditions, while others may read all of the conditions and then decide where to start.

Possible difficulties

- Selecting a number that matches only the first criterion
- Not matching the number against all criteria

Extension

- Pupils think of a number and make up criteria to match it, then give it to other pupils to solve.
- A one-digit number could be tried first, then a two-digit number.
- Conditions used can involve terms such as 'between', 'more than', 'less than' and 'place value'.
- Pupils can also be encouraged to come up with mathematical criteria of their own.

| 62 | 73 | 20 | 53 | 78 | 39 |

My number:

- *is between 65 and 95*
- *is less than 75*
- *has a 3 in the ones place*
- *is more than 68.*

1. My number is _____.

| 76 | 34 | 84 | 63 | 39 | 25 |

My number:

- *is between 21 and 72*
- *is more than 31*
- *has a 4 in the ones place*
- *is less than 35.*

2. My number is _____.

Problem-solving

To develop spatial visualisation in order to solve problems and to build a means of organising information in more complex problems.

Curriculum links

England (Year 2)
- Using and applying: Describe patterns and relationships involving shapes.
- Understanding shape: Identify shapes from pictures of them in different positions and orientations.

Northern Ireland (Key Stage 1)
- Processes in maths: Develop different approaches to problem solving.
- Shape and space: Make pictures using 2-D shapes.

Scotland (First)
- Properties of 2-D shapes: Explore simple 2-D shapes and how different shapes fit together.

Wales (Foundation)
- Skills: Develop a variety of mathematical approaches and strategies.
- Shape, position and movement: Make patterns of shapes and fit together shapes in various ways.

Materials

Tangram puzzles or cut-outs made from the template on page 57.

Note: Explain to pupils that the shapes drawn on pages 19–21 are not to scale.

Focus

These pages explore the use of tangrams to make shapes as well as the arrangements of shapes. Spatial thinking, as well as logical thinking and organisation, are involved as pupils investigate manipulating the pieces to form the various shapes. Being able to visualise in this way will help them solve many other problems in number, measurement, and chance and data, as well other spatial problems.

Discussion

Page 19
The first activities are designed for pupils to explore the relative sizes of the individual pieces and the ways in which the sides match to allow them to fit together. Practising this will help them with the more open-ended fourth task.

Page 20
These activities build on the comprehension developed on page 19 and help pupils to understand that many problems can be solved in more than one way.

Page 21
The first activity requires pupils to use logical reasoning and to extend their understanding of appraising pieces with matching sides to sorting out whether a design matches with a given shape or information. Pupils can match their pieces to see whether a pattern is possible or not. The first diagram requires six triangles and so cannot be made. The next diagram uses all seven pieces, with matching sides aligned, and so can be made. The third diagram requires three small triangles and so cannot be made. The last diagram uses only six pieces and requires pupils to use logical, organised thinking to match a complex shape.

Possible difficulties

- Not readily rotating shapes to find matching sides
- Not flipping the trapezium piece (the only non-symmetric piece) to give a different-looking shape
- Thinking there is only one possible solution

Extension

- Make the two shapes at the top of page 19 using only four tangram pieces.
- Pupils can investigate other tangram shapes.

Cut out the tangram pieces from the sheet your teacher gives you and use them to make each shape.

Use pieces 4, 5 and 7.

Use pieces 4, 5 and 6.

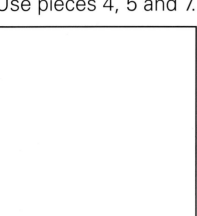

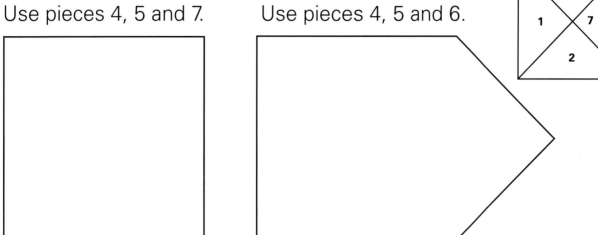

Use pieces 2, 5, 6 and 7.

Draw lines to show the pieces you used.

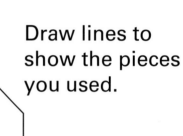

Make the shape. Use only three pieces.

Can you make it in any other ways?

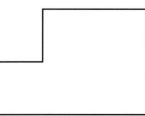

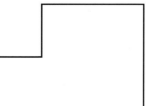

Cut out the tangram pieces from the sheet your teacher gives you and use them to make each shape.

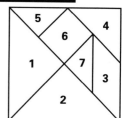

Use 2 pieces.
Draw the pieces you used.

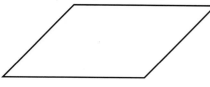

Use 3 pieces.
Draw the pieces you used.

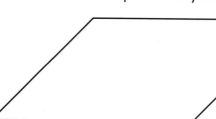

Use 3 pieces.
Draw the pieces you used.

Use 4 pieces.
Draw the pieces you used.

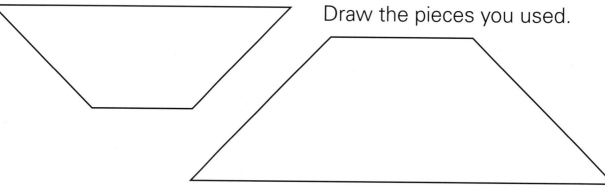

Use any of the pieces to make the shapes.

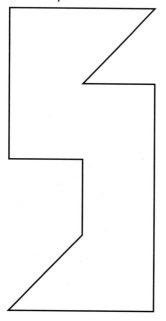
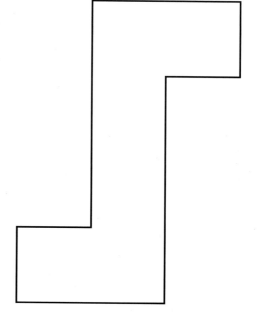

www.prim-ed.com   Prim-Ed Publishing®

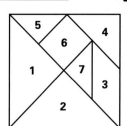

Cut out the tangram pieces from the sheet your teacher gives you and use them to make each shape.

Which of the shapes can be made by using all of the tangram pieces?

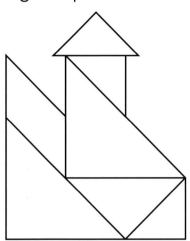

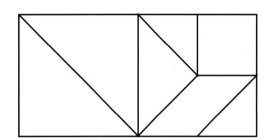

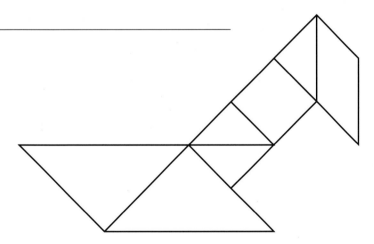

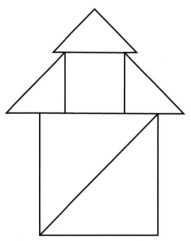

Use all of your pieces to make the shape.

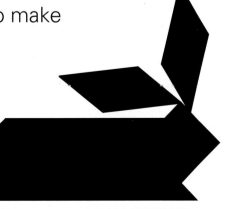

Problem-solving

To interpret and organise information in a series of interrelated problem statements.

Curriculum links

England (Year 2)
- Using and applying: Solve problems in the context of numbers.
- Using and applying: Identify the information needed to solve a problem.

Northern Ireland (Key Stage 1)
- Processes in maths: Develop different approaches to problem solving.

Scotland (First)
- Expressions and equations: Compare number relationships.

Wales (Foundation)
- Skills: Develop a variety of mathematical approaches and strategies.

Focus

These pages explore ways to arrange given numbers into problem situations so that the resulting stories make sense. Pupils need to read the stories carefully to work out which number goes where. The numbers are not listed in the order in which they are used in the story. To extend this concept, some questions require pupils to think of their own numbers to fit problem situations.

Discussion

Page 23

The first two problems require pupils to read and interpret the given situations and then place the numbers that are provided in the sentences so that the resulting story makes sense. Pupils need to make decisions about who is the oldest person and who is the youngest and use their understanding of 'group words' to make sense of the situations. The last problem uses the same story structure, but pupils are required to provide numbers of their own that will make appropriate stories.

Page 24

The problems on this page extend from the thinking used for page 23. The first situation must be read and interpreted so that the pupils use the numbers provided to produce a story that makes sense. The second problem uses the same story structure but asks pupils to think of their own numbers. The last problem extends this to a different situation, one in which pupils have to choose numbers without a set of 'rules' to follow. There is considerable leeway as to what numbers would make sense, but an understanding of the context is also needed; for example, to have 100 pupils in the class would not be likely, while 35 might be more reasonable.

Page 25

Here the idea of pupils choosing their own numbers to pose problems is extended to a more complex situation and is linked to the earlier notion of using a table to organise and analyse information. The various stories pupils write should be discussed and contrasted. The leading concept that should be understood by pupils is that a range of numbers can be used in each sentence (there is no one right answer).

Possible difficulties

- Placing the numbers in a story in the order in which they are listed rather than considering if they make sense.
- Not taking into account the context of the story when selecting numbers.
- Pupils having difficulty when trying to think of their own numbers for a story to make sense.

Extension

- Pupils should be encouraged to write further stories of their own and swap them with others in the class to solve.
- Pupils could write stories with and without numbers.

MISSING NUMBERS

Some numbers have been left out of the story. Put in the numbers so that the story makes sense.

| 6 | 11 | 9 |

1. Patty is the oldest child in her family.

   She is _____ years old.

   Helen is younger than Rina. Helen is _____ years old.

   Rina is _____ years old.

Some numbers have been left out of the story. Put in the numbers so that the story makes sense.

| 5 | 2 | 10 |

2. Roger bought a packet of socks.

   The packet has _____ pairs of socks.

   Altogether, Roger has _____ socks.

   He shopped for _____ hours.

Use your own numbers in the story so that it makes sense.

3. Roger bought a packet of socks.

   The packet has _____ pairs of socks.

   Altogether, Roger has _____ socks.

   He shopped for _____ hours.

Some numbers have been left out of the story. Put in the numbers given so that the story makes sense.

| **7** | **12** | **3** |

1. Mandy's school is _____ kilometres from her house.

   Her class has lunch at _____ o'clock.

   She is _____ years old.

Now use your own numbers so that the story makes sense.

2. Mandy's school is _____ kilometres from her house.

   Her class has lunch at _____ o'clock.

   She is _____ years old.

   What is the youngest age Mandy

   could be? _____

Choose your own numbers so that this story makes sense.

3. Haani's mother works _____ kilometres from their house.

   She works as a teacher and has _____ pupils in her class.

   Her pupils go home at _____ o'clock.

MAKE YOUR OWN STORY

Make up your own numbers to use in the story. Draw a picture of your story when you have finished.

1. Linda and Lisa are sisters.

   Linda is _____ years old.

   She is in Year _____ at school.

   Lisa is her older sister. Lisa is _____ years old.

   Lisa is in Year_____ at school.

   Linda and Lisa have a brother, Lenny.

   Lenny is younger than Lisa but older than Linda.

   Lenny is _____ years old.

2. Record how old each person is in the table below.

Linda	Lisa	Lenny

3. Draw a picture of your story.

Problem-solving

To solve problems involving money and make decisions based on particular criteria.

Curriculum links

England (Year 2)

- Using and applying: Solve problems involving addition and subtraction in the context of pounds.
- Knowing and using number facts: Derive and recall addition and subtraction facts.
- Calculating: Add or subtract mentally.

Northern Ireland (Key Stage 1)

- Processes in maths: Select the mathematics appropriate for a task.
- Processes in maths: Develop different approaches to problem solving.
- Number: Understand the operations of addition and subtraction and use them to solve problems.
- Number: Develop strategies for adding mentally.
- Number: Add and subtract money and solve money problems.

Scotland (First)

- Addition/Subtraction: Use addition and subtraction when solving problems.
- Money: Use money to pay for items and work out change.

Wales (Foundation)

- Skills: Develop a variety of mathematical approaches and strategies.
- Skills: Develop a variety of mental and written strategies of computation.
- Number: Calculate in a variety of ways.
- Number: Understand and use money.

Materials

Some pupils may need counters, play money or a calculator.

Focus

Pupils explore reading for information, obtaining information from another source (the picture) and using both to find solutions. The problems are about using money, making decisions based on money and comparing amounts of money, rather than addition or mental facts. Solutions can be obtained by using materials and comparing amounts. The item amounts have been kept small to assist with the problem-solving. Counters, blocks, play money or a calculator can be used if needed. This investigation lends itself to using a calculator and could be used to introduce calculator work or to extend work previously completed on a calculator.

Discussion

Page 27

Pupils read the items for sale and note how much each one costs. Pupils who are not familiar with money can still do the activity with a calculator. This investigation involves pupils reading for information and also getting information from another source—the toyshop. They need to remember what they are buying and then figure out how much it is, and in some cases to add and in others to compare amounts to see if they have enough money.

The last two questions have a number of possible solutions. Pupils might choose three items they would like and then add and compare only to discover they don't have enough money, while others may use choose the three cheapest items. Either way they need to compare money amounts and make decisions accordingly.

Possible difficulties

- Confusion with the £ symbol
- The concept of 'enough money' as oppose to an exact amount
- Not buying different items when necessary
- Thinking the exact amount of £10 has to be spent rather than not spending more than that amount

Extension

- Make a list of all the different ways pupils could spend their £10.
- In pairs, have pupils write other questions for the toy shop.

TOY SHOP

1. Nadia has £20. Does she have enough to buy the ball and the paint set? _____

2. Nathan has £15. Can he buy 2 balls and a truck? _____

3. Danielle has £30. She buys a cricket bat, a ball and 2 water pistols.

   How much money does she have left? _____

4. Minh has £15. He wants to buy 3 presents for his friends. Choose 3 things he can buy with his money.

   _____

   _____

5. If you had £20, what would you buy? _____

   _____

Problem-solving

To use spatial visualisation and logical reasoning to solve problems.

Curriculum links

England (Year 2)
- Using and applying: Describe patterns and relationships.
- Using and applying: Present solutions to problems in an organised way.

Northern Ireland (Key Stage 1)
- Processes in maths: Develop different approaches to problem solving.
- Processes in maths: Organise work and work systematically.
- Processes in maths: Recognise simple patterns and relationships.

Scotland (First)
- Patterns and relationships: Continue and devise repeating patterns.

Wales (Foundation)
- Skills: Develop a variety of mathematical approaches and strategies.
- Skills: Recognise patterns through practical activities.

Materials

Two-by-three grids with counters to model the problems.

Focus

These pages explore possible arrangements or combinations to determine all of the possibilities in a situation. Spatial thinking, as well as logical thinking and organisation, are involved as pupils investigate all likely arrangements and make sure that they do not repeat the possibilities. The acquisition of understanding the systematic logic needed to solve these problems will also assist in solving many other problems, not merely those that involve similar arrangements.

Discussion

Page 29

The example uses only one egg to show all of the possible arrangements that can be used. Extending this to placing four eggs is more complex and there is both the likelihood of coming up with the same arrangement more than once or of missing one or more possibilities. There are more egg cartons than needed.

Page 30

Using three eggs requires a systematic approach in order to find all the possibilities while avoiding duplication.

Page 31

Thinking and organisation similar to that used on page 29 is needed to find the paths the spider can take. Again, there are more webs drawn than are needed, but ensuring that a path is used only once may be more difficult than placing eggs differently. Travelling in and out of the centre of the web is needed, as well as traversing the outer lines.

Possible difficulties

- Not recognising that an arrangement has been used more than once.
- Using all of the egg cartons or spider webs, whether they are needed or not.

Extension

- Discuss the methods pupils used to systematically find all of the possibilities without omitting or repeating any. Contrast the different ways of thinking without necessarily favouring one over another.
- Extend the spider web problem by adding another outside web line.
- Investigate the egg carton problem further by using two brown eggs and two white eggs.

The egg carton has room for 6 eggs.

There are 6 ways you can put 1 egg into the tray.

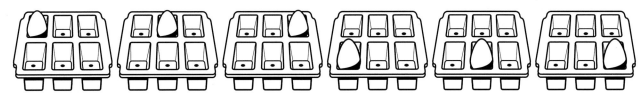

Amanda has an egg carton and 4 eggs.

1. Draw the different ways she can put the eggs into the egg carton. The first arrangement has been done for you.

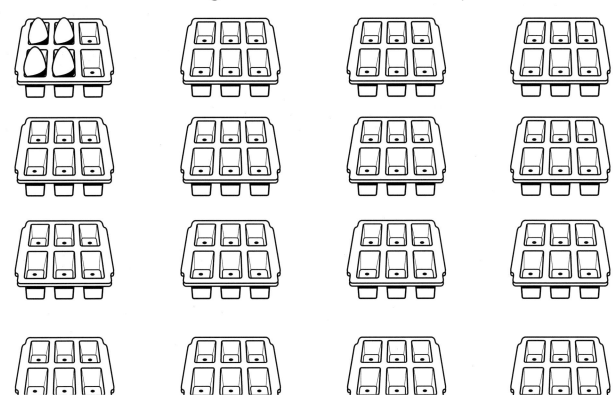

2. Did you use all of the egg cartons? _____

3. How many did you use? _____

EGG CARTONS 2

Jamie has an egg carton and 3 eggs.

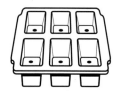 

1. Draw the different ways she can put the eggs into the egg carton. The first arrangement has been done for you.

 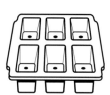  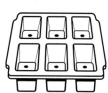

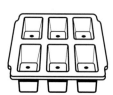  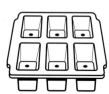 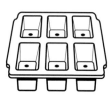

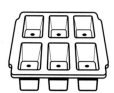 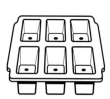 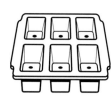 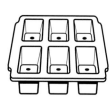

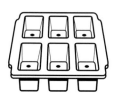  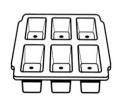 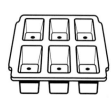

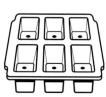 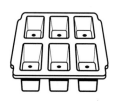 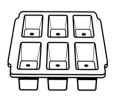 

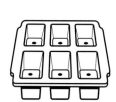 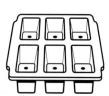 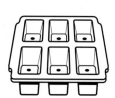 

2. Did you use all of the egg cartons? _____

3. How many did you use? _____

SPIDER WEBS

Help the spider catch the fly.

1. On each web, draw a different path from the spider to the fly. The spider can only run along each line once.

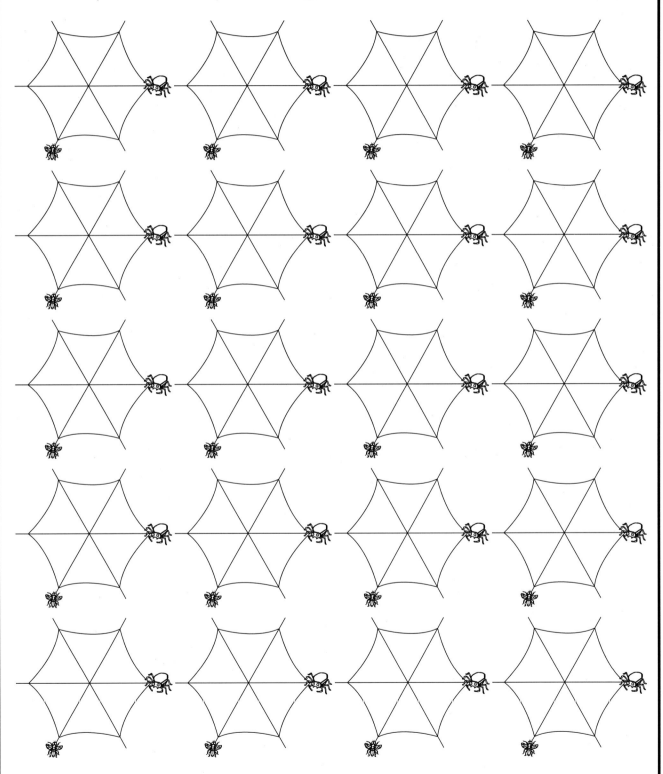

2. Did you use all of the webs? _____

Problem-solving
To identify and use information in subtraction problems.

Curriculum links
England (Year 2)
- Using and applying: Solve problems involving subtraction in the context of numbers.
- Using and applying: Identify and record the information or calculation needed to solve a problem.
- Knowing and using number facts: Derive and recall subtraction facts.
- Calculating: Add mentally.

Northern Ireland (Key Stage 1)
- Processes in maths: Select the mathematics appropriate for a task.
- Processes in maths: Develop different approaches to problem solving.
- Number: Understand the operation of subtraction and use subtraction facts.
- Number: Develop strategies for subtracting mentally.

Scotland (First)
- Subtraction: Use subtraction when solving problems.

Wales (Foundation)
- Skills: Develop a variety of mathematical approaches and strategies.
- Skills: Develop a variety of mental and written strategies of computation.
- Number: Calculate in a variety of ways.

Materials
Some pupils may need a place value chart or a calculator.

Focus
These pages explore word problems that require subtraction. Pupils need to determine what the problems are asking in order to find solutions. Analysis of the problems reveal that numbers must be identified and then subtracted correctly. Some problems may contain information that will not be needed or involve more than one subtraction to provide a solution. Problems involving subtraction as a comparison include the word 'more', which may lead to the problem being interpreted as addition.

Discussion
Page 33
The stories must be read carefully to see what information is needed. In the first three problems, the use of the word 'left' explicitly suggests subtraction. The fourth problem requires further interpretation of the language used to see what is needed, while the last problem involves a comparison of two different animals.

Page 34
Not all of the information is needed to find a solution. For example, in the last problem an understanding of the context shows that it is only the number of bikes that must be considered, not their colour.

There are different ways this problem can be solved. The number of bikes the shop had and the number sold can be totalled and then the subtraction carried out—the bikes sold are 10, leading to simple subtraction and addition. Alternatively, the number of red bikes sold and the number of black bikes sold could be found by subtraction and totalling the remaining amounts.

Page 35
This problem involves a larger amount of information, with a number of questions arising from it. A careful reading of the information is needed to sort out which numbers must be subtracted. In each case, the initial number is known and the amounts can be subtracted in turn to obtain the answer.

When the first question states that three roses are picked each day, the focus of the problem changes, since the question is asking how many times can this happen.

The final problem combines arrangements and is similar to the problem on page 30. However, the problem also involves subtraction, since it is asking how many ways items can be subtracted from eight.

Possible difficulties
- Unable to identify the need to subtract to find a solution.
- Adding rather than subtracting, or simply stating one of the written numbers as the result.
- Confusion in identifying which numbers must be subtracted.
- Lack of ability to subtract readily and accurately.

Extension
- Ask pupils to write problems for other pupils to complete, using the problems on the worksheets as a model.

1. There were 16 jelly beans in the jar. During the day, 7 were eaten. How many jelly beans are left?

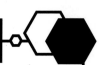

_____

2. The farmer has 27 cows in a paddock. He moves 11 cows to another paddock. How many cows does he have left in the first paddock?

_____

3. There are 27 kangaroos drinking at the waterhole. 8 kangaroos hop away. How many kangaroos are left drinking at the waterhole?

_____

4. The last carriage on the train had 13 people. At the station, 7 people got off. How many people were still on the train?

_____

5. The farmer has 11 sheep and 17 goats. How many more goats than sheep does the farmer have?

_____

1. The minibus has enough seats for 16 children and 1 driver. There are 9 children on the bus. How many more children can fit on the bus?

_____

2. Craig has 24 stickers, Alex has 37 stickers and Henrick has 48 stickers. How many more stickers does Henrick have than Craig?

_____

3. Julie caught 31 fish and 4 crabs. She threw 14 small fish and 2 small crabs back into the water. How many fish did she keep?

_____

4. The bicycle shop has 12 red bikes and 16 black bikes. It sells 3 red bikes and 7 black bikes. How many bikes are left?

_____

ROLAND'S ROSES

The rosebush has 13 roses on it. Roland picked 2 roses one day, 4 roses the next day and 3 roses on the third day.

1. How many roses are left on the bush? _____

   If he picks 2 roses each day for 3 days, how

   many are left on the bush? _____

   If he picks 3 roses each day, for how many days

   can he pick roses? _____

   If he picks a bunch of 6 roses, how many are left? _____

   If he picks 2 bunches of 6 roses, how many are left? _____

ANGELA'S POTS

Angela has 8 pot plants.

Inside	Outside

2. If 2 pots are kept outside, how many are kept inside?

   _____

   List the different ways Angela can arrange her plants inside and outside.

Problem-solving

To use diagrams, make predictions and logically reason

Curriculum links

England (Year 2)
- Using and applying: Describe patterns and relationships and make predictions.

Northern Ireland (Key Stage 1)
- Processes in maths: Develop different approaches to problem solving.
- Processes in maths: Recognise simple patterns and relationships and make predictions.

Scotland (First)
- Patterns and relationships: Continue and devise repeating patterns.

Wales (Foundation)
- Skills: Develop a variety of mathematical approaches and strategies.
- Skills: Investigate repeating patterns and relationships and make simple predictions.

Materials

Drawing materials and calculator or counting blocks, if needed

Focus

These pages explore how many pegs are needed to hang various amounts of bedsheets. Pupils are required to make predictions and use diagrams to gather the information needed to find solutions. The problems could be completed using multiplication; however, they can also be done by using a diagram and counting, with addition and counters, by using basic doubles facts or with a calculator.

Discussion

Page 37
Some pupils may be able to visualise the bedsheets and pegs and find a solution, while others may need to draw bedsheets and count the pegs. This information can then be used to figure out the amount for nine sheets. Also, some pupils may be able to predict the number of pegs needed in the activity involving six sheets and draw a diagram to confirm the amount.

The next activity extends this concept, with the bedsheets now joined together so, rather than four pegs for two bedsheets, there are now three pegs for two sheets. Again, the pupils could draw the bedsheets and then draw the pegs to count them. This same diagram could also be used to work out the questions regarding 10 and 16 sheets, rather than drawing a new diagram. Some pupils may be able to predict the number of pegs based on the previous activity and then draw a diagram to confirm this.

Possible difficulty

- Drawing two pegs on each bedsheet when it should be three pegs per two sheets

Extension

- Make a table listing how many bedsheets and pegs are needed when there are two pegs per sheet and a table listing how many pegs are required when it is three pegs per two sheets.

SHEETS AND PEGS

The hotel is hanging out its bedsheets to dry. Each sheet needs 2 pegs.

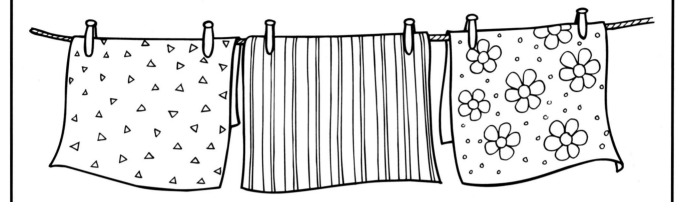

1. How many pegs are used if 6 bedsheets are hung out? _____

   What about 9 sheets? _____

There are too many bedsheets and not enough pegs. They decide to join the sheets together and use 3 pegs for 2 sheets.

2. How many pegs would be used to hang 8 bedsheets? _____

   What about 10 sheets? _____

   What about 16 sheets? _____

Problem-solving

To organise data and make predictions.

Curriculum links

England (Year 2)
- Using and applying: Describe patterns and relationships and make predictions.

Northern Ireland (Key Stage 1)
- Processes in maths: Develop different approaches to problem solving.
- Processes in maths: Recognise simple patterns and relationships and make predictions.

Scotland (First)
- Patterns and relationships: Continue and devise repeating patterns.

Wales (Foundation)
- Skills: Develop a variety of mathematical approaches and strategies.
- Skills: Investigate repeating patterns and relationships and make simple predictions.

Materials

Calculator or counting blocks, if needed

Focus

These pages explore different ways data can be analysed and recorded. In each situation, diagrams, tables and lists can be used to organise and sort the data in order to make predictions for further analysis and exploration. Visualisation, as well as logical reasoning, is involved in these investigations.

Discussion

Page 39

Analysis of the problems reveals that the distance travelled entails movement back and forth. The first problem involves climbing four metres up and then slipping two metres back, so each day the distance travelled is two metres. As the pipe is 12 metres high, it will take exactly six days to reach the top.

The next problem is similar but in this case the time will not be exact. As the well is 23 metres deep and the travel distance is three metres per hour, it will take eight hours to reach the top, with not all of the last hour needed. During the last hour a distance of two metres must be travelled, not three metres. The last problem entails a distance travelled of three metres every one and a half hours on the way up, and three metres every hour and 10 minutes on the way down. Again, the time will not be exact.

Page 40

Pupils need to organise the data to calculate the possibilities. This could be done by using a list or a table or even with counting materials. There are three possible thin-base pizzas and three possible thick-base pizzas. The extension to three types of pizza base should enable some pupils to immediately see that there will again be three thin-base, three thick-base and three wholemeal-base pizzas.

Other pupils may be able to see a pattern emerge. Some pupils will be able to look at the last question regarding three bases and three toppings and be able to just answer it based on the previous question since, again, it will be the same.

Page 41

This investigation builds on the previous work on page 37. Pupils look at the diagram of the stories and visualise how many pins are needed if there are ten stories in two separate rows. Some pupils may be able to look at the diagram and use that to solve it, while others may need to complete the drawing. The problem is extended in the next activity, in which the rows are now joined together, reducing the number of pins needed.

Possible difficulties

- Not using a table or list to manage the data
- Not working out how far was really travelled when moving forward and backward
- Not realising that a ham and cheese pizza is the same as a cheese and ham pizza
- Not remembering that the pupils' stories can be overlapped to save using pins

Extension

- Make a table showing how far was travelled by each animal per day/hour.
- Explore what would happen if you used three/four types of bases and three/four toppings.
- Explore different arrangements of artwork—two rows with six paintings each and four rows with three paintings each.

1. A drainpipe is 12 metres long. Each day, a snail climbs 4 metres up the drainpipe but then slips back 2 metres overnight. How long will it take for the snail to reach the top of the drainpipe?

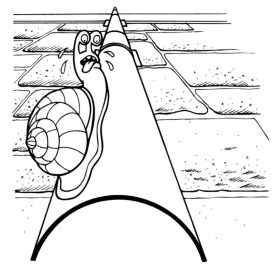

_____

2. A green frog is at the bottom of a well. Each hour, he climbs 5 metres but then slips back two metres. If the well is 23 metres deep, how long will it take the frog to get out of the well?

_____

3. A tree snake climbs up and down a tree to its nest. Each hour it climbs up a distance of 3 metres and then rests for 30 minutes. If the tree is 14 metres high, how long will it take the snake to reach its nest?

_____

When climbing down the tree from the nest, it slides 3 metres every hour and then rests for 10 minutes. How long will it take for the snake to reach the ground?

_____

PIZZA PARTY

Alex and Nicky are making pizzas for a party. They decide to make each pizza different.

We have thin bases and thick bases.

We have ham, cheese and pineapple.

1. Write all of the different pizzas they can make if they only use 1 topping per pizza.

THIN BASE	THICK BASE
_____	_____
_____	_____
_____	_____

2. How many pizzas can they make? _____

3. What happens if they use 2 toppings per pizza? | **more** | **less** | **same** |

4. Write all of the different ways they can make pizzas using 2 toppings.

THIN BASE	THICK BASE
_____	_____
_____	_____
_____	_____

5. What happens if they also have wholemeal pizza bases?

_____

6. How many pizzas can they now make using only 1 topping?

_____

7. How many pizzas can they now make using all 3 toppings?

_____

Rick is helping his teacher pin up some stories.

1. He is putting up 10 stories. How many pins does he need? _____

Melinda is helping her teacher pin up the class's artwork. She has 12 paintings that she is going to pin up in 3 rows, with 4 paintings in each row.

2. How many pins does she need? _____

Problem-solving

To visualise relationships shared by two-dimensional shapes.

Curriculum links

England (Year 2)
- Using and applying: Describe patterns and relationships involving shapes.
- Understanding shape: Identify shapes from pictures of them in different positions and orientations.

Northern Ireland (Key Stage 1)
- Processes in maths: Develop different approaches to problem solving.
- Shape and space: Make pictures using 2-D shapes.

Scotland (First)
- Properties of 2-D shapes: Explore simple 2-D shapes and how different shapes fit together.

Wales (Foundation)
- Skills: Develop a variety of mathematical approaches and strategies.
- Shape, position and movement: Make patterns of shapes and fit together shapes in various ways.

Materials

Pattern block shapes, grid paper or cut-out shapes

Focus

These pages explore making shapes and arrangements of shapes. Spatial and logical thinking and organisation are involved, as pupils investigate all possible arrangements and extensions. Being able to visualise patterning of this form will help pupils solve many other problems, including those involving number, measurement, and chance and data, as well as other spatial problems.

Discussion

Page 43

Some pupils may need to physically manipulate the shapes to find the combinations that make the rectangle. This may involve rotating and/or flipping some of the pieces. Other pupils may be able to visualise the shapes and realise which two combine to make the rectangle. Encourage pupils to explore rotating and flipping the pieces to come up with other shapes.

Page 44

This activity requires the use of pattern block shapes or triangular grid paper. A number of different pieces can be used to cover the hexagon. When using pattern block shapes, there are eight possible arrangements if you include the hexagon piece as one of the ways to cover it. Encourage pupils to explore rotating and flipping the pieces when trying to find combinations of shapes that will fit together to cover the hexagon. Some pupils will need to try different pieces and then discard them, while others may be able to visualise various possibilities.

Page 45

This activity requires the use of pattern block shapes or triangular/square grid paper. As the shapes do not have the lines drawn showing which pieces are needed, pupils will need to explore the different pattern block shapes in order to see which pieces make each shape. Encourage pupils to make predictions and give a verbal description of their findings. Pupils may need an extra copy of the sheet to answer Question 4.

Possible difficulties

- Difficulty rotating or flipping the pieces as needed
- Unable to visualise possible pieces to make the shapes

Extension

- Investigate other shapes that can be made and/or covered with the pattern block shapes.

MAKING SHAPES

Look at the rectangle and the pieces below it.

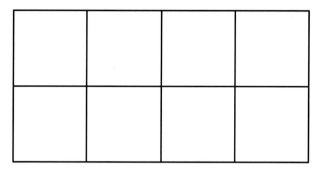 

(a)  (b) 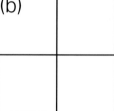 (c) 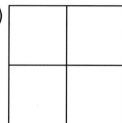 (d)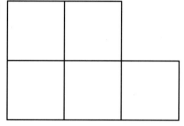

Which pieces fit together to make the rectangle? _____

Cut out the pieces and check. What other shapes can you make?

Find this pattern block shape.

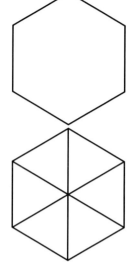

Cover it with six triangles.

What other shapes or pattern blocks can you use to cover it?

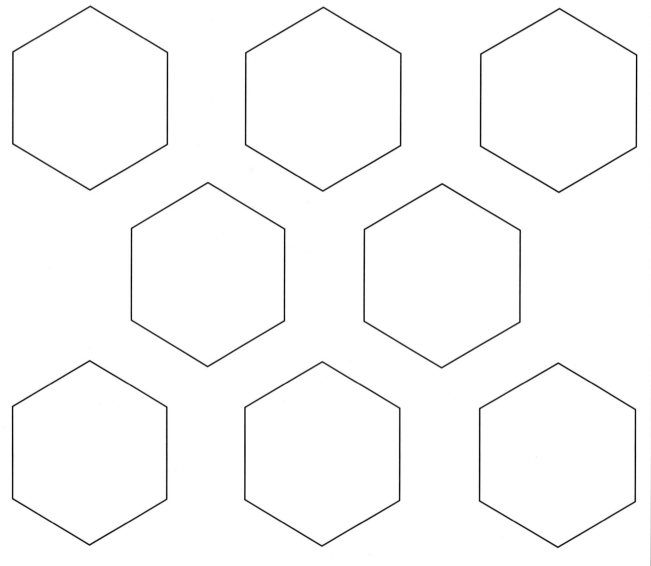

Did you find 8 different ways? _____

MORE SHAPES

Making shapes with pattern blocks

Look at the shapes below.

Make each shape using only four pattern blocks.

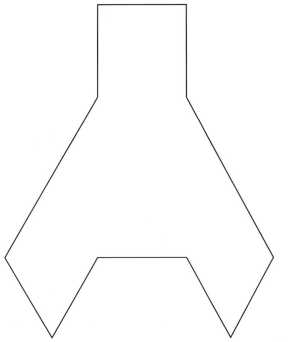

Draw lines to show how you made them. Colour the different parts.

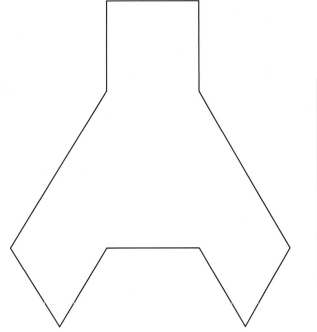

Can you make each shape using five blocks? _____

Draw lines to show and colour the different parts.

Problem-solving

To analyse and use information in addition and subtraction problems.

Curriculum links

England (Year 2)
- Using and applying: Solve problems involving addition and subtraction in the context of numbers.
- Using and applying: Identify and record the information or calculation needed to solve a problem.
- Knowing and using number facts: Derive and recall addition and subtraction facts.
- Calculating: Add and subtract mentally.

Northern Ireland (Key Stage 1)
- Processes in maths: Select the mathematics appropriate for a task.
- Processes in maths: Develop different approaches to problem solving.
- Number: Understand the operations of addition and subtraction and use addition and subtraction facts.
- Number: Develop strategies for adding and subtracting mentally.

Scotland (First)
- Addition/Subtraction: Use addition and subtraction when solving problems.

Wales (Foundation)
- Skills: Develop a variety of mathematical approaches and strategies.
- Skills: Develop a variety of mental and written strategies of computation.
- Number: Calculate in a variety of ways.

Materials

Counters, blocks or calculators

Focus

These pages explore word problems that require addition and subtraction. Pupils must determine what the problem is asking and, in many cases, carry out more than one step in order to find solutions. Analysis of the problems reveals that different items may need to be added, while other problems contain additional information that is not needed.

Materials can be used to assist with the calculation if necessary, as these problems are about reading for information and determining what the problem is asking, rather than computation or basic facts.

Discussion

Page 47

Careful reading of each problem is needed to determine what the question is asking. In some cases, more information is provided than is needed, and some problems contain amounts that are not required to find the solution. Some problems have more than one step, and both addition and subtraction are needed at times. There are a number of ways to find a solution and pupils should be encouraged to explore and try different possibilities of arriving at a solution.

Page 48

On this page, pupils are told that some problems involve addition and some involve subtraction and that only the subtraction problems must be solved. This requires a careful analysis of each story to determine what the problem is asking and whether addition or subtraction is needed to find a solution.

This activity shifts the focus from trying to find 'an answer' to understanding the importance of determining what a problem is asking.

Page 49

This investigation involves information about an aviary and a number of interrelated questions arising from it. The situation begins with a number of birds either flying around, in nests or on the ground.

Using this information as a base, pupils are required to keep track of new information and use it to answer the subsequent questions. The number of birds change to meet new criteria, with some birds landing and some birds flying.

Possible difficulties

- Inability to identify when to add and when to subtract
- Confusion over the need to carry out more than one step to arrive at a solution
- Using the total amount listed rather than just the numbers needed

Extension

- Pupils could write their own problems and give them to other pupils to solve.

46
Problem-solving in mathematics
www.prim-ed.com
Prim-Ed Publishing®

1. The fruit shop sold 46 punnets of strawberries on Monday, 62 punnets on Tuesday and 73 punnets on Wednesday. How many punnets were sold altogether?

_____

2. On Friday, 17 bags of oranges and 9 bags of lemons were sold. On Saturday, 19 bags of oranges and 6 bags of lemons were sold. How many bags of oranges were sold?

_____

3. The fruit shop has 24 trays of mangoes. On Saturday, 6 trays were sold and, on Sunday, 8 trays were sold. How many trays were not sold?

_____

4. On Tuesday, 24 bags of potatoes were sold. On Wednesday, 6 bags of onions and 19 bags of potatoes were sold. On Thursday, 12 bags of potatoes were sold. How many bags of potatoes were sold?

_____

Read the problems. Some involve addition and some involve subtraction. Solve ONLY the subtraction problems.

1. There are 27 koalas in a tree. 16 koalas are sleeping. How many koalas are not sleeping?

   _____

2. 18 koalas are eating gumleaves. 4 more koalas start eating leaves. How many koalas are eating gumleaves?

   _____

3. 35 koalas are sleeping in the tree. 9 koalas wake up. How many koalas are still sleeping?

   _____

4. 37 adult koalas are in the tree. 8 koalas have a baby on their back. How many koalas do not have a baby on their back?

   _____

5. 26 koalas are sleeping in the tree. 9 more koalas go to sleep. How many koalas are sleeping?

   _____

BIRD AVIARY

In the aviary, 43 birds are flying around, 19 birds are on the ground and 13 birds are in their nests.

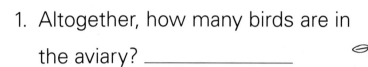

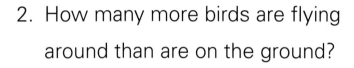

1. Altogether, how many birds are in the aviary? _____

2. How many more birds are flying around than are on the ground?

_____

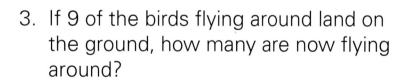

3. If 9 of the birds flying around land on the ground, how many are now flying around?

_____

4. How many are now on the ground?

_____

5. All of the birds in their nests leave them to land on the ground to feed. How many birds are on the ground?

_____

Problem-solving

To solve problems involving time.

Curriculum links

England (Year 2)

- Using and applying: Solve problems involving addition in the context of numbers and measures.
- Knowing and using number facts: Derive and recall addition facts.
- Calculating: Add mentally.

Northern Ireland (Key Stage 1)

- Processes in maths: Select the mathematics appropriate for a task.
- Processes in maths: Develop different approaches to problem solving.
- Number: Understand the operation of addition and use addition facts.
- Number: Develop strategies for adding mentally.

Scotland (First)

- Addition: Use addition when solving problems.

Wales (Foundation)

- Skills: Develop a variety of mathematical approaches and strategies.
- Skills: Develop a variety of mental and written strategies of computation.
- Number: Calculate in a variety of ways.

Focus

This page explores finding and interpreting information from a map. Analysis of the map shows the time it takes to walk various distances. Pupils are required to interpret this information and record it in the table. The table can then be used to help with the questions. Some destinations are not direct and most have more than one possible route.

Discussion

Page 51

- Hut to lake: If it takes two hours to walk there, it will take two hours to walk back.

- Hut to cave past the forest: Involves going past the forest on the way to the cave, rather than walking the direct route past the lake, which is used on the return journey.

- Waterfall to lake: There is no direct route to the lake from the waterfall, and Alice would need to go via the cave or the hut. Discussion could centre on why one way would be better than another; for example, the route past the hut is much shorter, but the route past the cave might provide a nicer view or a better path.

Possible difficulties

- Inability to read the map and list the information in the table
- No understanding of the concept of 'there and back again'
- Not knowing what to do when there is no direct route

Extension

- Pupils can use the map and write other questions for others to solve.

ALICE'S ISLAND

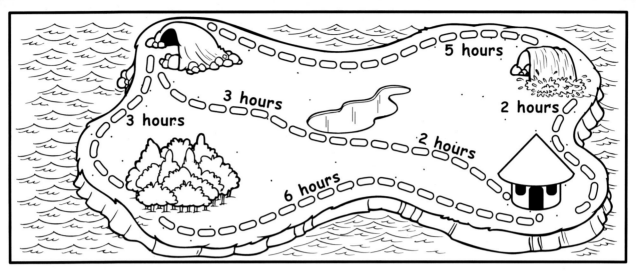

1. Fill in the walking times.

Track	Hours	Track	Hours
hut to lake		forest to cave	
hut to cave		forest to waterfall	
hut to forest		waterfall to lake	
hut to waterfall		lake to cave	
waterfall to cave			

2. How long would it take Alice to walk from her hut to the lake and

   back again? _____

3. Alice walked from her hut to the cave. She went past the forest
   on her way to the cave. How long did it take her?

   _____

4. How long would it take her if she returned home past the lake?

   _____

5. How long would it take for Alice to walk from the waterfall to the

   lake? _____

SOLUTIONS

Note: *Many solutions are written statements rather than simply numbers. This is to encourage teachers and students to solve problems in this way.*

BLOCKS .... **page 3**

1.

RB	RG	RY
BR	BG	BY
GR	GB	GY
YR	YB	YG

2. 12

3.

RBG	RYB	BRG	GBR	GYR	YBG
RBY	RYG	BRY	GBY	GYB	YBR
RGY	BGR	BYG	GRB	YRB	YGR
RGB	BGY	BYR	GRY	YRG	YGB

4. 24

GRID FUN .... **page 4**

1. Answers will vary; for example:

R	B	G
B	G	R
G	R	B

2. One diagonal is all the same colour and the other is one of each colour.

3. Answers will vary; for example:

R	B	G
G	R	B
B	G	R

MORE BLOCKS .... **page 5**

1. Answers will vary; for example:

R	B	G	Y
B	G	Y	R
G	Y	R	B
Y	R	B	G

2. (a) Answers may vary and include: one diagonal is all the same colour and the other has only two colours.
   (b) Centre square is of two repeated colours.

---

3. Answers will vary; for example:

R	B	G	Y
B	R	Y	G
G	Y	R	B
Y	G	B	R

BLOCK STREET .... **page 7**
Answers will vary.

HOW MANY? 1 .... **page 9**
1. Anne
2. 42
3. 58
4. Sunday
5. Jane

SWAP CARDS .... **page 10**
1. Julie
2.

Mark	John	Carla
53	43	72

3. Carla
4. John

MAGIC SQUARE .... **page 11**
1. (a)

6	1	8
7	5	3
2	9	4

Magic number: 15

(b)

8	1	6
3	5	7
4	9	2

Magic number: 15

IN THE GARDEN .... **page 13**
1. 29 leaves
2. 24 birds
3. 65 cows
4. 86 mangoes

SOLUTIONS

Note: *Many solutions are written statements rather than simply numbers. This is to encourage teachers and students to solve problems in this way.*

HOW MANY? 2 .... **page 14**
1. 7 books
2. 10 shirts
3. 48 people
4. 14 feathers

HOW MANY? 3 .... **page 15**
1. 32 ducks
2. 23 black goats
3. 14 guinea pigs
4. 23 kangaroos

WHAT'S MY NUMBER? .... **page 17**
1. 73
2. 34

TANGRAMS 1 .... **page 19**
1. (a)

(b)

 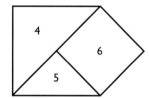

(c)

 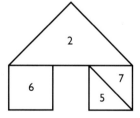

2. As above
3.

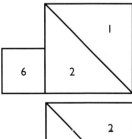

4.

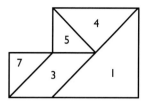

TANGRAMS 2 .... **page 20**
1. (a)

 or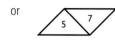

(b)

(c)

 or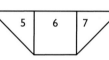

(d)

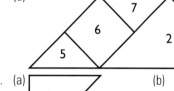

2. (a) 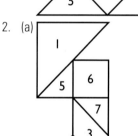 (b)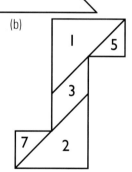

TANGRAMS 3 .... **page 21**
1. (a)

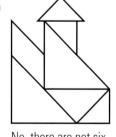 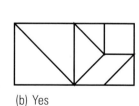

No, there are not six triangles.

(b) Yes

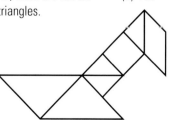

(c) No, there are only two small triangles.

SOLUTIONS

Note: Many solutions are written statements rather than simply numbers. This is to encourage teachers and students to solve problems in this way.

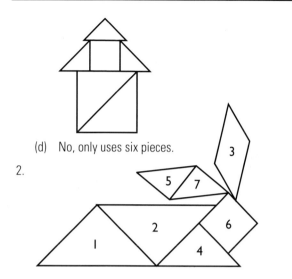

(d) No, only uses six pieces.

2.

MISSING NUMBERS .... page 23
1. (a) 11
   (b) 6
   (c) 9
2. (a) 5
   (b) 10
   (c) 2
3. Answers will vary.

MORE MISSING NUMBERS .... page 24
1. (a) 3
   (b) 12
   (c) 7
2. Answers will vary.
3. Answers will vary.

MAKE YOUR OWN STORY .... page 25
1. Answers will vary.
2. Answers will vary.
3. Teacher check

TOY SHOP .... page 27
1. Yes. They cost £15.
2. No. They cost £16.
3. £4
4. Answers will vary; e.g. truck, car, water pistol.
5. Answers will vary; e.g. cricket bat and ball.

EGG CARTONS 1 .... page 29
1.

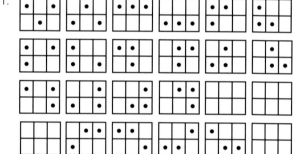

2. No
3. 15

EGG CARTONS 2 .... page 30
1.

2. No
3. 20

SPIDER WEBS .... page 31
1. Answers will vary; for example:

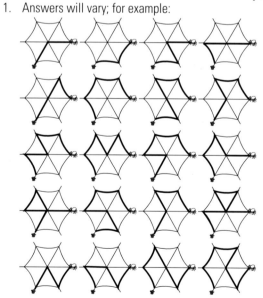

2. Answers will vary

SOLUTIONS

Note: Many solutions are written statements rather than simply numbers. This is to encourage teachers and students to solve problems in this way.

1. 9 jelly beans
2. 16 cows
3. 19 kangaroos
4. 6 people
5. 6 goats

1. 7 children
2. 24 stickers
3. 17 fish
4. 18 bikes

1. (a) 4 roses
   (b) 7 roses
   (c) 5 days (but can only pick 1 rose on day 5)
   (d) 7 roses
   (e) 1 rose
2. (a) 6 pots
   (b)

Inside	Outside
0	8
1	7
2	6
3	5
4	4
5	3
6	2
7	1
8	0

1. (a) 12 pegs
   (b) 18 pegs
2. (a) 9 pegs
   (b) 11 pegs
   (c) 17 pegs

1. 6 days
2. 8 hours (or 7 and a bit hours)
3. (a) 7 hours (or 6 and a bit hours)
   (b) 6 hours (or 5 and a bit hours)

1.

THIN BASE	THICK BASE
ham	ham
cheese	cheese
pineapple	pineapple

2. 6 pizzas
3. same
4.

THIN BASE	THICK BASE
ham and cheese	ham and cheese
ham and pineapple	ham and pineapple
cheese and pineapple	cheese and pineapple

5. It allows for 3 more options.
6. 9 pizzas
7. 3 pizzas

1. 24 pins
2. 20 pins

1. b and d
2. Teacher check

1. Answers will vary; for example:

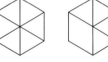

2. Answers will vary.

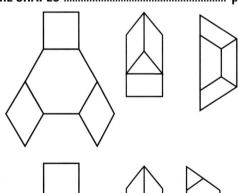

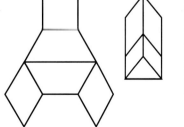

3–4. Teacher check

SOLUTIONS

Note: *Many solutions are written statements rather than simply numbers. This is to encourage teachers and students to solve problems in this way.*

AT THE FRUIT SHOP .... **page 47**
1. 181 punnets
2. 36 bags of oranges
3. 10 trays
4. 55 bags

KOALA CORNER .... **page 48**
1. 11 koalas are not sleeping
2. addition (do not answer)
3. 26 koalas
4. 29 koalas do not have a baby on their back
5. addition (do not answer)

BIRD AVIARY .... **page 49**
1. 75 birds
2. 24 birds
3. 34 birds
4. 28 birds
5. 41 birds

ALICE'S ISLAND .... **page 51**

1.

Track	Hrs	Track	Hrs
hut to lake	2	forest to cave	3
hut to cave	5	forest to waterfall	8
hut to forest	6	waterfall to lake	4
hut to waterfall	2	lake to cave	3
waterfall to cave	5		

2. 4 hours
3. 9 hours
4. 5 hours
5. 4 hours (shorter route)

TANGRAM RESOURCE PAGE

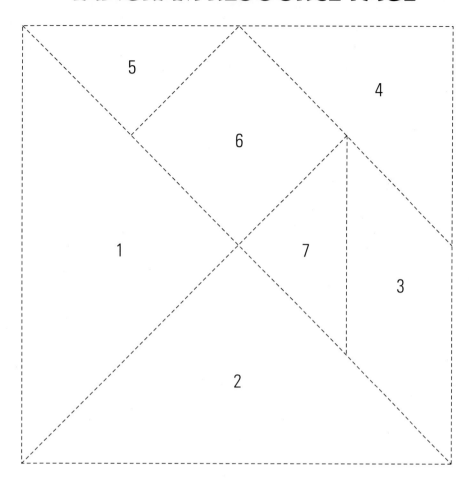

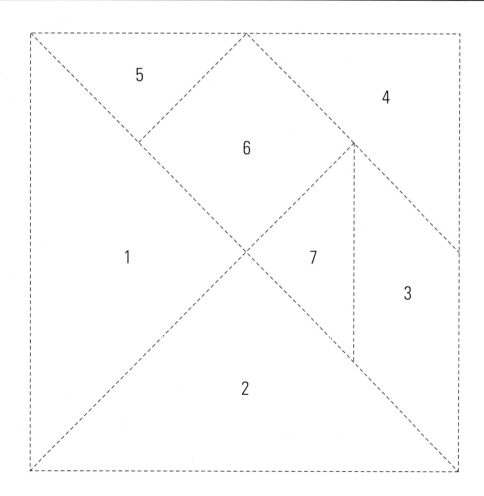

10 mm x 10 mm GRID RESOURCE PAGE

15 mm x 15 mm GRID RESOURCE PAGE

TRIANGULAR GRID RESOURCE PAGE

TRIANGULAR ISOMETRIC RESOURCE PAGE

SQUARE ISOMETRIC RESOURCE PAGE